D0927452

Gautrek's Saga and other medieval tales

Gautrek's Saga and other medieval tales

Translated with an introduction by
Hermann Pálsson and Paul Edwards

New York · NEW YORK UNIVERSITY PRESS
London · UNIVERSITY OF LONDON PRESS LTD

Library of Congress Catalog Card No: 68–16829

Set in 'Monotype' Fournier
Printed in Great Britain by
Cox and Wyman Ltd, Fakenham

CONTENTS

123771

INTRODUCTION

When people speak of the Icelandic sagas, they normally have in mind works from the two principal groups, the *Sagas of Icelanders* or *Family Sagas*, and the *Kings' Sagas*. The stories translated here come not from these two groups, but from a third, less well known, called the *Legendary Sagas*; and one of our objects is to demonstrate that these deserve greater attention, and have their place in the narrative tradition of medieval Europe. But before we discuss the stories in this volume, something must be said about the two major groups of sagas, since we shall be pointing to affinities between these and the *Legendary Sagas*.

The widely ranging literature of medieval Iceland owes its fame largely to a number of great prose epics on native themes. The late 13th century author of *Njal's Saga*, the most remarkable of these epics, recreated the way of life of a host of people who had been dead for nearly three hundred years, with such skill that we might be reading an eye-witness account of these remote events; and so permanent are the qualities of the narrative that the responses of a modern reader will probably not differ very greatly from those of the original audience. But while *Njal's Saga* is regarded as the most magnificent of the sagas, it should be borne in mind that many of its outstanding features are shared with other *Sagas of Icelanders* (as this genre is usually called): a fascination with the past, a narrative style of dramatic verbal economy, a keen insight into human motives, and an author delighted with the creative power of his imagination. Sagas of a similar stature to *Njal's Saga* include *Laxdæla Saga*, a study in conflicts of love and jealousy, conciliation and revenge; *Egil's Saga*, a portrait of the uncompromising, complex poet and killer; *Grettir's Saga*, the hero's struggle against fate and an implacable society; *Hrafnkel's Saga*, *Eyrbyggja Saga*, and many more.

Written between the 12th and 14th centuries, the *Sagas of Icelanders* describe life in native Iceland in the 10th and 11th centuries, shortly after the emergence of Iceland as a nation. One of the reasons for their success may be their concern with historical themes. This is not to say

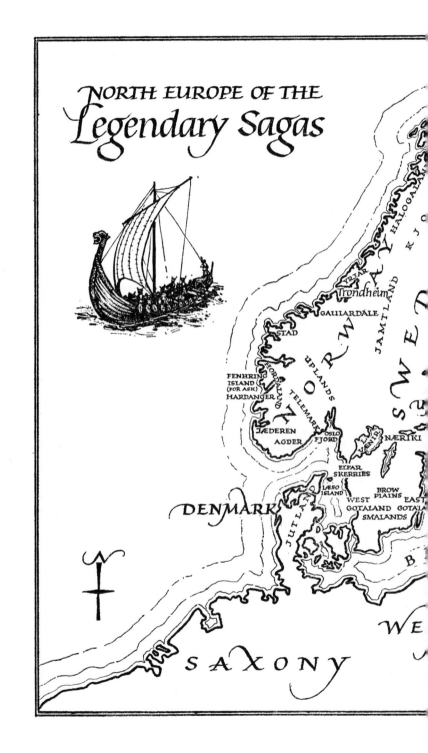

NORTH EUROPE OF THE
Legendary Sagas

Trondheim

GAULARDÂLE

STAD

FENHRING
ISLAND
(FOR ASK)
HARDANGER

JÆDEREN
AGDER

HÖRÐALAND

TELEMARK

UPLANDS

NORWAY

JAMTLAND

HALOGALAND

KJŌ

SWED

OSLO
FJORD

VENIR

NÆRIKI

ELFAR
SKERRIES

LÆSO
ISLAND

BROW
PLAINS

WEST
GOTALAND

EAST
GOTALA

SMALANDS

B

DENMARK

JUTLAND

SAXONY

WE

FINNMARK

PERMIA

Novgorod

RUSSIA

Kiev

that their exclusive purpose was to record historical facts, for it is well known now, as it must have been to 13th century audiences, that they contain a number of fictional elements. But the social, historical and geographical setting of the sagas imposed certain disciplines on their authors, restricting their freedom to go beyond what audiences would accept as proper embellishments to the history of their own immediate ancestors.

Though some original features of Icelandic society had been distorted by the establishment of Christianity and the subsequent struggle for wealth and power, its structure was still basically the same in the 13th century as it had been in the 10th. In many cases, the important farmers for whom the sagas were written were still living on the farms where their forefathers had established their homes at the time of the settlement of Iceland around A.D. 900. Legal custom was still in many ways the same as it had been in the 10th century, though it had been modified to suit the new faith. The coming of Christianity in the year A.D. 1000 had failed to break up the social structure, and pagan values and beliefs often survived the acceptance of Christianity. These sagas, then, were acted against too familiar backgrounds, and the people of the 13th century had too great a knowledge of and respect for their 10th-century ancestors, for the author to be able to tamper with history, geography, and customary beliefs. Of course, the authors did not hesitate to introduce new characters into their stories or to invent dialogue, and so clothe with flesh the skeleton of a tradition. But the stories had to sound plausible to a knowledgeable audience, and all that might be incongruous or anachronistic had to be avoided: in fact, the author had rather less licence than the historical novelist of our own time.

Many of these features of the *Sagas of Icelanders* are also found in some of the sagas on broader Scandinavian themes in *Heimskringla,* written by the Icelander Snorri Sturluson (1179-1241). This monumental work follows the history of the throne of Norway from legendary times down to A.D. 1177. It is a masterly survey of the evolution of royal power, but told in human rather than political terms, with many brilliantly-written narrative episodes. A large part of it deals with the period of the Vikings, where incidentally it touches on various aspects of early British history, and it has provided Norway with a lasting image of her own beginnings, though many of the details undoubtedly originated in Snorri's fertile imagination. There was more scope here for invention, particularly in the shadowy regions of early history where it becomes increasingly hard to distinguish men from gods.

When we speak of the historical basis of the *Sagas of Icelanders* and the *Kings' Sagas*, we must make a qualification: to put it simply, we can say that for the authors of these sagas, native history only started in the second half of the 9th century, about the time the earliest Icelandic settlements were made by Norwegian emigrants. Anything before about the year 850 tended to be regarded as belonging to pre-history, to the legendary past, and this has to be borne in mind when we try to evaluate the sagas from an historical point of view. It is as if the learned men of Iceland could only reach back in time with any confidence to the beginnings of the society in which they themselves lived. Before the emergence of the Icelandic nation, their vision of the past fades into the uncertain world of legend and myth.

So it was the heroic period of the Settlement and the century which followed, often called the Saga Age, to which the Icelanders looked with so much nostalgia, and indeed continued to look even down to the present time. The memory of this period was cherished by native writers from the 12th century onwards, and the saga authors and the historians of the early 12th century had access to reliable traditions about life in Iceland right back to the early days of the Settlement. Thus, for example, Ari the Learned (1067-1148), author of the *Book of Icelanders (Íslendingabók)* and co-author of the *Book of Settlements (Landnámabók)* which proudly gives the names, with a wealth of genealogical and other detail, of about four hundred major settlers, used an informant who was born in 1023 and died in 1111 at the age of eighty-eight. She could remember some of the outstanding people who figure in the sagas, including her own father who was born in 963 and died in 1031. It was in fact quite easy for this intelligent woman to describe to the historian the record of her own family from as far back as the time of the Settlement. One of her great-grandfathers had emigrated from Norway to Iceland in 962, and one of her great-great-grandfathers, the founder of the family, had emigrated to Iceland in 884. Well-informed people like this woman provided the 12th-century historian with a firm unbroken link with the past. For this reason, it is not surprising that the period is described in the sagas so accurately and with such vitality. The same applied to the history of Norway during this period. In a lost work of Ari the Learned there was an account of the lives of the kings of Norway, Denmark and England during the years covered by his *Book of Icelanders*, from 870 to 1120. For the history of the English kings he undoubtedly used written sources, but for Norway and Denmark he had to rely on oral information. Now one of his informants knew a man who could remember as far back as the killing of Earl Hakon by his slave in 995, an incident referred to in the opening chapter of *Thorstein Mansion-Might's Story* in this volume. And Ari himself had been fostered by a farmer who had known King Olaf the Holy (ruler of Norway from 1016 to 1030) and could even remember being baptized at the age of three in 999.

We recognize, then, the firm historical basis for much of the material in the *Sagas of Icelanders* and the *Kings' Sagas*. But for the authors of the *Legendary Sagas* in this volume, who wanted to write about earlier periods, the problems were different and so were the results. Reliable traditions could only take the author back as far as the middle of the 9th century, though there were plenty of historically untrustworthy tales about more remote eras. Those who wanted to look beyond the beginnings of Icelandic society would turn to pagan poetry, to genealogies – there are several in the works of Ari, one of them tracing lines as far back as the gods – and to oral stories handed down for generations.

Before we come to these legendary sources, once again it should be stressed that the acceptance of Christianity in Iceland did not mark the same break in native tradition as might have been expected. The Icelandic historians took great pride in their pagan past, so it is not strange that a considerable corpus of pagan poetry has survived. Particularly notable are the poems dealing with mythological and legendary themes, now usually gathered under the general heading, *The Poetic Edda*. Snorri Sturluson, whom we have already mentioned, retold some of these in another of his major works, *The Prose Edda*. Further evidence of Snorri's interest in the remote past is his *Ynglinga Saga* (the early section of *Heimskringla*, and based chiefly on 9th-century poems), describing the legendary history of the royal house of Sweden and, in the final chapters, of Norway too, from the time of the god Odin down to the early 9th century. It seems likely that the author of *Bosi and Herraud* (see the opening sentences of the story), was influenced by Snorri's *Ynglinga Saga*, where Odin is called King of Sweden, and is said to have travelled from Asia. Here as elsewhere in the legendary literature, we are unsure whether men have become gods, or gods have been turned into men. *Gautrek's Saga*, the first story in this volume, has an affinity with yet another source of legendary materials, the late 12th-century legendary history of Denmark, *Skjöldunga Saga*, which now exists only in a Latin summary and an Icelandic fragment. Finally, yet another early work relevant to three of the sagas here – *Gautrek's Saga*, *Thorstein Mansion-Might's Story*, and *Helgi Thorisson's Story* – is Saxo Grammaticus' massive *Danish History*. Saxo, who died in 1216, paid tribute, as had a Norwegian contemporary Theodricus, to the Icelanders' historical learning. Saxo states emphatically that he had made use of their saga treasures (*thesauri historiarum*), and the first nine books of his *History* deal with the legendary and mythological past of Denmark. It is to these books, and in particular Books VI and VIII, that we look for parallels to our Icelandic tales.

The *Legendary Sagas*, from which the five stories in this volume come, originated in the 12th century, though the type continued to be written for many centuries after. Two of the five – *Thorstein Mansion-Might's Story* and *Helgi Thorisson's Story* – are associated on one level with the historical King Olaf Tryggvason who ruled from 995 to 1000; but on another with the legendary King Godmund of Glasir (i.e. Shining) Plains, who also appears in *Bosi and Herraud*; *Bosi and Herraud* and the two remaining sagas translated here have a wholly pagan setting. There is little to indicate that the authors of the *Legendary Sagas* wanted their audiences to identify the tales with any particular period, but a few of the characters in them can be given tentative dates. Both Harald War-tooth and Gautrek are mentioned in pedigrees in the *Book of Settlements*, and, as far as these can be relied on, the two kings should have lived around the years 700 to 800. Starkad is also mentioned in the same source, and is said to have been associated with the court of a Swedish king who, if the genealogies are to be trusted, lived around the year 750. But as we have tried to make clear, the historical content of these legendary sagas is comparatively slight. They were intended primarily as entertainments – one might almost say as escape literature – and in this connection it may be significant that their popularity seems to have increased as conditions in Iceland deteriorated, with the loss of independence in 1262 and the increasing economic burdens of subsequent centuries. But in spite of their escapist function, the *Legendary Sagas* have retained more of the qualities of the great saga tradition than has, perhaps, been generally recognized.

Like the history, the geography of these sagas is deliberately hazy. Not only are the heroes followed through Scandinavia and across the Baltic into Eastern Europe: we are taken deeper, into Tartary and the arctic wastes of Permia, west to England and south to the Mediterranean. We even hear of characters from India and Ethiopia. Going beyond geography, we travel to the Otherworld of pagan Scandinavia, to Geirrodstown, Gjallandi Bridge, Noatown and Valhalla of the *Poetic Edda*, and to the ambiguous Glasir Plains, the barren region lying between the geographical *Ultima Thule* of Permia, and the unearthly Geirrodstown. In one of the sagas not included here, *Samson's Saga*, there is a brave attempt at rationalizing some of the weird geographical features of the legendary tales:

> Glasir Plains are situated to the east of Giantland, which lies to east and north of the Baltic and extends in a north-easterly direction. Then there is the land known as Jotunheim, inhabited by giants and monsters, and from Jotunheim to Greenland there extends a land called Svalbard (i.e. Spitzbergen).

To the modern reader of these tales, as to the medieval, much of the interest will lie in the strangeness of the material and settings. But there is more to them than a kind of Gothic sensationalism, and the fantastic elements are continually being blended with the realistic. So, for example, we have a drinking horn called Grim the Good, with a carved head on it that talks and gives advice: but this is taken very much for granted, and as a result the talking head begins to assume a humanity of its own:

Then a number of musical instruments came playing into the hall, and two men, both rather smaller than Thorstein, carried in Grim the Good between them. All the people got to their feet, then knelt down before him, but there was an ugly look about Grim.

Geirrod spoke to Godmund, 'Take Grim the Good and let this toast bind you to your pledge.'

Godmund went over to Grim, took his gold crown off, put it on Grim's head, and whispered into his ear as Thorstein had instructed him. Next, he poured the poisonous drink into his shirt. When he had drunk in this way to King Geirrod's health, he kissed the point of the horn and Grim was taken away from him with a smile on his face.

We can recognize similar features in the career of Bosi. His amorous feats and his fondness for occasional arbitrary violence might remind the reader of one or two popular modern fictional figures – as we have said, these sagas are in a sense escapist literature. At the same time, Bosi in context is rather more than a simple erotic Superman. There is an accumulating strain of exaggeration throughout the saga, which in relation to the blunt hero produces a rather clownish effect at times. As a result, the whole thing appears increasingly to be done tongue-in-cheek, almost as a mock-epic and culminating in epic-farce, the grotesque parody of a legendary battle with monsters with which the saga ends.

The narrative method also displays at times a considerable subtlety and complexity, for example in the skilful exploitation of flashbacks in *Egil and Asmund*, and the control of several related plots in which characters cross at intervals from one narrative line to another. These skills allow the author to elaborate on what might otherwise have been simple folk narratives, and as a result that hoary chestnut, the abduction and rescue of a captive princess, is merely the beginning and the end of *Egil and Asmund*, the interest lying principally in what happens in between.

A blurring of outlines between the normal and the fantastic is characteristic of the tales. The world in which they take place has clear affinities with that of folk-lore and the ballads. The forests are haunted by fairies and demons that often appear, as in folk tradition, because a tree is cut or nuts are gathered – the old spirits of the trees are offended, it seems, though this is never made explicit. Here one finds the taboos of folk-lore against speaking to, or taking food from these spirits, or having any kind of sexual relationship with their women. So Helgi's blinding by Ingibjorg, arbitrary though it may appear, is a traditional punishment for breaking the taboo, as in the ballad, *Tam Lin*:

> 'Had I kend, Thomas,' she says,
>   'A lady wad hae borrowd thee,
> I wad hae taen out thy twa grey een,
>   Put in twa een o tree.'

Thus the fantasy of the tales is often rooted in folk tradition, but sometimes, too, one recognizes an historical basis even to their wilder moments. The account of the backwoodsmen in *Gautrek's Saga* who jumped to their deaths over Family Cliff whenever anything out of the ordinary happened is by no means as incredible as it sounds. Bede records something very similar in his *History of the English Church and People*, iv.13. (translated by Leo Sherley-Price, Penguin Classics, 1955):

> No rain had fallen in the province for three years prior to his (i.e. Bishop Wilfred's) arrival, and a terrible famine ensued which reduced many to an awful death. It is said that frequently forty or fifty emaciated and starving people would go to a precipice, or to the sea shore, where they would join hands and leap in, to die by the fall or drowning.

On the whole, then, the atmosphere of these tales is not so much fantastic, as shifting continually between the fantastic and the credible and human, a feature incidentally of some of the most striking parts of the great sagas, notably *Grettir's Saga* and *Eyrbyggja Saga*. Nor is the handling of fantastic or supernatural scenes merely sensational, as we have seen. In *Gautrek's Saga*, the gods who dominate Starkad's fortunes are a mythical machinery by means of which the human and tragic dilemma of Starkad is presented; the chaotic battle at the end of *Bosi and Herraud* seems designed as a deliberate piece of anti-heroic comedy; and the incident of the suicides from Family Cliff in *Gautrek's Saga*, even if we knew nothing of Bede and other historical sources, would remain a striking demonstration of neurotic fears in an isolated community.

All the same, the world of these legendary tales is as a rule different from that of the *Sagas of Icelanders* in certain important respects. In the latter, everything tends to be more sharply focused, events and characters stand out clearly in the cold, familiar light of the authors' native land. But in the *Legendary Sagas*, echoes from a remote past and distant lands constantly reach us. If the effects are sharply defined they often have the sharp definition of the dream or nightmare, and the apparently clear outlines of what has appeared to be normal life suddenly become indistinct.

Although the hero may belong to a definite place in Norway or Sweden, the moment he moves away from his home he begins to defy the laws of nature. Inside the mound or the forest he finds a world infested with dwarfs and giants: he passes through a belt of mist, and fairy women greet him from the mythical Glasir Plains, the home of the enigmatic King Godmund. Starkad goes into a wood with his foster-father, who suddenly turns out to be Odin and introduces Starkad to a whole Pantheon of gods.

These two figures, Starkad and Godmund, are particularly memorable, and it might be worth while to say a little about them at this point. If Godmund comes from the borderland of the Otherworld, Starkad stands on the verge of this one. He is the foster-son of a disguised Odin, and in contact with a multitude of spirits and monsters. But he is also the very human epitome of the tragic saga-hero, a man to be compared with Grettir whose life was said to show how great talents and good luck are two quite different things. Both Starkad and Grettir are human and vulnerable, yet they are also marked out from ordinary men and their sufferings are more keenly defined. Grettir, like Starkad an outstanding warrior and poet, is doomed by the incompatability of his nature with the society in which he finds himself. In the story of Starkad the same point is being made in mythological terms, when the hero's character is ordained by the caprice of the gods. In both cases, the mood of the tale is dictated by the heroism of a man whose choices continue to be made in the face of what appears to be predestined. Characteristically, the choice is between two evils, equally unacceptable.

B

In Starkad's case, it lies between loyalty to his foster-father, Grani Horse-Hair (who also happens to be Odin himself), and to his lord, King Vikar. He accepts the public shame which he must bear if he kills Vikar simply because he knows that the gods demand a sacrifice and someone must make it. His terrible destiny is shown to him: but, heroically, he chooses to embrace it.

One of the chief sources for the story of Starkad is Saxo's *Danish History*, and Saxo is also one of our chief informants on another outstanding figure of these tales, the mysterious Godmund of Glasir Plains. Godmund is clearly a semi-mythical figure, and lives in the waste land near the impassable river that divides our world from the Otherworld. In *Thorstein Mansion-Might's Story*, where Godmund pays a visit to Geirrod of Geirrodstown, there is an echo of Thor's journey to the same place as it is told by the 10th-century poet Eilif and later, in the 13th-century, by Snorri in his *Prose Edda*. According to both Eilif and Snorri, Geirrod was a giant hostile to the gods, and Thor's visit was far from friendly. On the way, Thor had to ford a formidable river called Vimur, which obviously corresponds to the river Hemra in our story. The ambiguous qualities of Godmund in these tales can perhaps be at least partially explained by Godmund's place in pagan tradition on one hand, and in Christian tradition on the other. To Thorstein Mansion-Might he is a friendly figure, an enemy of the forces of evil which are represented by Geirrod, and only too happy to get the assistance of Thorstein. When he and Thorstein go their separate ways, Godmund sends valuable gifts to King Olaf, and in addition 'Godmund asked Thorstein to come and visit him, and they parted the best of friends'. It is clear, in fact, that Godmund has plenty of respect for the Christian King Olaf's 'luck', and at another point in the tale he promises that if Thorstein becomes his man he will not interfere with Thorstein's faith. Very different is the picture of Godmund which emerges from *Helgi Thorisson's Story*. In spite of his gestures of friendship to King Olaf, it is made clear that Godmund is evil and dangerous, and in the end, as a warning no doubt to those who mix in this sort of company, it is Godmund's sister who gouges out Helgi's eyes. Finally, in *Bosi and Herraud*, while Godmund is a slightly ludicrous enemy, his sister Hleid ends up as the beloved wife of Herraud.

The ambivalent attitude to pagan figures in some of the sagas is not so surprising when we think of the cultural climate in which their authors lived. Although it has proved impossible to date these sagas with any degree of accuracy, there seem to be good reasons for believing that in their present form, they may have been written in the early part of the 14th century. By then, saga-writing had a long history behind it and was very much a time-honoured part of the national life. On the whole, the church took a sensible and sympathetic view of sagas, even when they dealt with pagan themes. As one medieval commentator shrewdly put it, 'while you are listening to a saga being read aloud, you are not likely to think any sinful thoughts.' Thus even profane sagas could serve an edifying Christian purpose, if only in a passive sort of way. Though the author of *Helgi Thorisson's Story* feels obliged to preach against heathenism, as a rule the saga author did not necessarily feel compelled to do this. He could, if he so wished, not only set his story in a completely pagan context, but even describe the events as if seen through pagan eyes. So, though the author may at times impose Christian values on the tale, he can at others create the impression of a story not conceived in a Christian mind, but growing out of the very time in which it is set, miraculously preserved for later generations.

Any translator of medieval literature is likely to find himself up against a few serious obstacles. He is often made uncomfortably aware that literary taste is an impermanent thing. Even more recent works than these early 14th-century tales have failed to retain their value and interest for the modern reader. Our task, however, has been comparatively easy, for in all these stories the emphasis is upon a lively narrative, and the manner of telling the story is unlikely to seem odd or offensive to modern taste. So we hope that the reader will discover more than an antiquarian interest in these examples of the narrative art practised with such skill in Iceland, six or seven hundred years ago.

BIBLIOGRAPHICAL NOTE

Since this translation is intended for the general reader, we thought it inappropriate to include a detailed bibliography. However, any reader wishing to learn something of the background to the legendary sagas will find Margaret Schlauch's *Romance in Iceland* (Allen and Unwin, 1934) a valuable and highly-readable book. For a more general account of the sagas, see Professor E.O.G. Turville-Petre's *The Heroic Age in Scandinavia* (Hutchinson, 1951) and, more specifically on the mythology, his *Myth and Religion of the North* (Weidenfeld and Nicolson, 1964).

NOTE ON THE TRANSLATIONS

The five sagas in this volume first appeared in print in the early part of
the 19th century, and their manuscript tradition goes back to the 14th
and 15th centuries (see below). The present translations are based on
the edition in *Fornaldarsögur Norðurlanda*, ed. Guðni Jónsson (Reyk-
javik, 1950), but we have supplied new titles to the chapters.

There are two extant versions of *Gautrek's Saga*, the earliest of
which survives in a single vellum MS dating from the 15th century and,
like most other legendary sagas, in a number of later paper MSS as well.
It is this early version which we have translated here. As far as we know
this is the first complete English translation of this saga. One of the
sources used by the author was a (12th century?) poem attributed to
Starkad, and since its contents are to a large extent repeated in the prose
we decided to relegate all but the last two groups of verses of the poem
to footnotes (see *Starkad's Verses* p. 53).

Bosi and Herraud (*Bósa saga ok Herrauðs*), of which there is again
no previous English translation, is preserved in two versions, and here
also we have based our translation on the earlier version. It may be of
some interest to note that the later version is in a bowdlerized form,
presumably made by some prudish scribe who objected to the erotic
role played by Bosi. The precise significance of the runes in chapter five
is obscure, although there can be little doubt as to the value of individual
symbols. The first six runes are the equivalents of *R A TH K M U*, and

the following clusters consist of the runic letters *I S T I*; the last sign ⌐̇

is uncertain. It is possible that the whole string of runic letters may
represent a riddle, but we must confess ourselves as baffled by this as
was Hring in the story.

Egil and Asmund ('Egils saga einhenda ok Ásmundar saga berserk-
jarbana') survives in three vellum MSS, the earliest of which dates
from the end of the 14th century and has been used as the basis for
all printed editions. This is the first complete version of the saga in
English.

Thorstein Mansion-Might's Story ('þorsteins þáttr bæjarmagns') survives in a 15th century vellum MS. *Helgi Thorisson's Story* ('Helga þáttr þórissonar') is preserved in the so-called *Flateyjarbók*, a magnificent vellum codex made during the years 1382–95 for a wealthy farmer in the north of Iceland. These stories were both translated by Miss Jacqueline Simpson in her saga collection *The Northmen Talk* (Phoenix House, 1965). In this same volume Miss Simpson has also provided a translation of certain selected passages from *Gautrek's Saga* and *Egil and Asmund*.

We have chosen to translate rather than transliterate a number of 'invented' names when the meaning seemed to demand this. In our glossary, however, we have given in brackets the Icelandic forms of all such names.

We are indebted to Mrs Betty Radice for reading these translations in manuscript and making several useful suggestions.

Edinburgh   Hermann Pálsson
May 1966   Paul Edwards

Gautrek's Saga

1. IN THE BACKWOODS

This is the start of an amusing story about a certain King Gauti. He was a shrewd sort of man, very quiet, but generous and outspoken. King Gauti ruled over West Gotaland, lying east of the Kjolen Mountains between Norway and Sweden; the Gota River separates Gotaland from the Uplands. In that part of the world there are immense forests, very difficult to get about in except when the ground is frozen.

This king we're talking about, Gauti, used to go into these forests with his hawks and hounds, for he was keen on hunting and got a great deal of pleasure from it.

At this time there were plenty of people living deep in the forests, as a good many settlers had cleared the land to make their homes right away from the world. A number of these backwoodsmen had turned from society because of some misdeed or other, or else had cleared out to avoid the consequences of youthful escapades or adventures; they thought the best way of protecting themselves against people's scoffing and sneering was to get completely away from it all, and so they lived out the rest of their lives without seeing another human being apart from their own companions. As these men had gone to live right off the beaten track, hardly anybody ever came to visit them, unless from time to time someone who happened to lose his way in the forest might stumble on their homes, and even so, he would often wish that he'd never set foot there.

This King Gauti we've been talking about started out with his retainers and his finest hounds to hunt deer in the forest. The king sighted a fine stag and set his heart on getting it, so he unleashed his hounds and began chasing hard after it. This went on all day, and by evening he had lost all his fellow huntsmen and was deep into the forest. He realized that he wouldn't be able to get back to them, as it was already dark and he'd covered so much ground during the day. Besides this, he'd hit the stag with his spear, and it had stuck fast in the wound. He didn't on any account want to lose the spear if he could possibly help it, since it seemed to him a great humiliation to surrender one's weapon. Gauti had been hunting so hard that he'd thrown off all his clothes except for his underwear. He'd lost his socks and shoes, and his legs and feet were badly torn by stones and branches, but still he had not caught up with the stag. By now it was night and very dark, and he had no idea where he was going, so he stopped to listen if he could hear anything, and after a little while he heard the bark of a dog. It seemed most likely that where a dog barked there would be people about, so he walked on in the direction of the sound.

Shortly afterwards he saw a small farmstead, and standing outside was a man with a woodcutter's axe. When he saw the king coming closer, the man pounced on the dog and killed it.

'This is the last time you'll show a stranger the way to our house,' he said. 'It's obvious, this man's so big he'll eat up all the farmer has once he gets inside. Well, that won't ever happen if I can help it.'

The king heard what the man said and smiled to himself. It occurred to him that he wasn't at all suitably dressed for sleeping out; on the other hand, he wasn't certain what sort of hospitality he would be offered if he waited for an invitation, so he walked boldly up to the door. The other man ran into the doorway with the idea of keeping him out, but the king forced his way past him into the house. He came into the living-room, where he saw four men and four women, but there wasn't a word of welcome for King Gauti. So he sat down.

One of them, evidently the master of the house, spoke up. 'Why did you let this man in?' he asked the slave at the door.

'I wasn't a match for him,' said the slave, 'he was so powerful.'

'What did you do when that dog started barking?' said the farmer.

'I killed the dog,' said the slave, 'I didn't want it to lead any more roughs like this to the house.'

'You're a faithful servant,' said the farmer, 'and I can't blame you for this awkward situation that's cropped up. It's difficult to find the proper reward for the trouble you've taken, but tomorrow I'll repay you by taking you along with me.'

It was a well-furnished house and the people were good-looking but not particularly big. It struck the king that they were frightened of him. The farmer ordered the table to be laid, and food was served. When the king saw that he wasn't going to be invited to share the meal, he sat

down at the table next to the farmer, picked up some food and settled
down to eat. When the farmer saw this, he stopped eating himself and
pulled his hat down over his eyes. Nobody said a word. After the king
had finished eating, the farmer pushed up his hat and ordered the
platters to be cleared from the table . . . 'since there's no food left there
now,' he said.

The king lay down to sleep, and a little later on one of the women
came up to him and said, 'Wouldn't you like me to give you a bit of
hospitality?'

'Things are looking up now you're willing to talk to me,' said the
king. 'Your household seems a pretty dull one.'

'Don't be surprised at that,' said the girl. 'In all our lives, we've
never had a single visitor before. I don't think the master is too pleased
to have you as a guest.'

'I can easily compensate him for all that he spends on my account,'
said the king, 'as soon as I get back to my own home.'

'I'm afraid this queer business will bring us something more from
you than compensation,' said the woman.

'I'd like you to tell me what you and your family are called,' said the
king.

'My father's called Skinflint,' she said, 'and the reason is, he's so mean
he can't bear to watch his food stocks dwindle or anything else he owns.
My mother's known as Totra because she'll never wear any clothes
unless they're already in tatters. She has the idea that this is very sound
economics.'

'What are your brothers called?' asked the king.

'One's called Fjolmod, another Imsigull, and the third Gilling,' she
said.

'What about you and your sisters?' asked the king.

'I'm called Snotra, because I'm the most intelligent. My sisters are
called Hjotra and Fjotra,' she said. 'There's a precipice called Gillings
Bluff near the farm, and we call its peak Family Cliff. The drop's so
great there's not a living creature could ever survive it. It's called Family
Cliff simply because we use it to cut down the size of our family whenever something extraordinary happens, and in this way our elders are
allowed to die straight off without having to suffer any illnesses. And

then they can go straight to Odin, while their children are spared all the trouble and expense of having to take care of them. Every member of our family is free to use this facility offered by the cliff, so there's no need for any of us to live in famine or poverty, or put up with any other misfortunes that might happen to us.

'I hope you realize, my father thinks it quite extraordinary, your coming to our house. It would have been remarkable enough for any stranger to take a meal with us, but this really is a marvel, that a king, cold and naked, should have been to our house. There's no precedent for it, so my father and mother have decided to share out the inheritance tomorrow between me and my brothers and sisters. After that they're going to take the slave with them and pass on over Family Cliff on the way to Valhalla. My father feels that's the least reward he could give the slave for trying to bar your way into the house, to let the fellow share this bliss with him. Besides, he's quite sure Odin won't ever receive the slave unless he goes with him.'

'I can see that you're the most eloquent member of your family,' said the king, 'and you can depend on me. I take it you're still a virgin, so you'd better sleep with me tonight.'

She said that was entirely up to him.

In the morning when the king woke up, he said, 'I'd like to remind you, Skinflint, that I was barefoot when I came to your house, so I wouldn't mind accepting a pair of shoes from you.'

Skinflint made no reply but gave him a pair of shoes. All the same he pulled out the laces first. The king said:

'Skinflint gave me
a pair of shoes,
but held the laces back.
I tell you a miser
can never give
a gift without a snag.'

After that the king got ready to go, and Snotra came to see him off.

'I'd like to ask you to come with me,' said King Gauti, 'I've an idea our meeting may have certain consequences. If you have a boy, call him

Gautrek; it'll remind you of me and all the trouble I've caused your family.'

'I think you're pretty near to the mark,' she said. 'But I shan't be able to go along with you now, as it's today my parents divide their property between me and my brothers and sisters. When that's done my father and mother intend to move on over Family Cliff.'

The king said good-bye to her and told her to come and see him whenever she felt like it. Then he went on his way until he came up with his men, and now he took it easy.

2. OVER THE CLIFF

But to get on with the story, when Snotra came back to the house, there was her father squatting over his possessions.

'What an extraordinary thing to happen,' he said, 'a king has paid us a visit, eaten us out of house and home and then taken away what we could least afford to lose. It's clear to me that we won't be able to stay together any longer as one family since we're reduced to poverty. That's why I've gathered together all my things. And now I'm going to divide them up between my sons. I'm going to take my wife along to Valhalla, and my slave as well, since it's the least I can do to repay him for his faithful service, to let him go there with me.'

'Gilling is to have my fine ox, to share with his sister Snotra. Fjolmod and his sister Hjotra are to have my bars of gold, Imsigull and his sister Fjotra all my cornfields. And now I want to implore you, my children, not to add to the family, so that you'll be able to preserve what you've inherited.'

When Skinflint had said all he wanted, the family climbed up to Gillings Bluff. After that the young people helped their parents to pass on over Family Cliff, and off they went, merry and bright, on the way to Odin.

Now that the young people had taken over the property, they decided they'd better set things right. So they cut some wooden pegs and used them to pin pieces of cloth round their bodies so that they couldn't touch each other They felt this was the safest method of controlling their numbers.

When Snotra realized she was going to have a baby, she loosened the wooden pins that held her dress together, so that her body could be touched. She was pretending to be asleep when Gilling woke or stirred in his sleep. He stretched out his hand and happened to touch her cheek.

Once he was properly awake, he said 'Something terrible has happened, I'm afraid that I've got you into trouble. You seem to be much stouter now than you used to be.'

'Keep it to yourself as long as you can,' she said.

'I'll do no such thing,' he said, 'once there's been an addition to our family there wouldn't be a hope of hiding it.'

Not long after, Snotra gave birth to a beautiful boy. She chose a name for him and called him Gautrek.

'What a queer thing to happen,' said Gilling, 'there's no hiding this any longer. I'm going to tell my brothers.'

'Our whole way of life is being threatened by this remarkable event,' they declared. 'This is indeed a serious violation of our rule.'

Gilling said:

'How stupid of me
to move my hand
and touch the woman's cheek.
It doesn't take much
to make a son
if that's how Gautrek was got.'

They said it wasn't his fault, particularly since he'd repented and was wishing it had never happened. He said he'd willingly pass on over Family Cliff, and added that this little affair might be only a beginning. His brothers told him to wait and see whether anything else would happen.

Fjolmod used to herd his sheep all day, carrying the gold bars with him wherever he went. One day he fell asleep and was woken up by two black snails crawling over the gold. He got the idea that the gold had been dented where it was really only blackened, and he thought it greatly diminished.

'It's a terrible thing,' he said, 'to suffer such a loss. If this should happen once more I'll be penniless when I go to see Odin. So I'd better pass on over Family Cliff just to cover myself in case it happens again. Things have never looked so black, not since my father handed me out all this money.'

He told his brothers about his remarkable experience, and asked them to share out his part of the property. Then he added:

'Scrawny snails
have swallowed my gold,
everything goes against me.
Stripped of my wealth,
I snivel and sulk,
now all my gold's been gobbled.'

Then he and his wife went up to Gillings Bluff and passed on over Family Cliff.

One day Imsigull was inspecting his cornfields. He saw a bird called the sparrow – it's about the size of a tit. He thought the bird might have caused some serious damage, so he walked round the fields till he saw where the bird had picked a single grain from one of the ears. Then he said:

'The sparrow's done
dire devastation
to Imsigull's field of corn.
He ravaged an ear
and gobbled a grain;
What grief to the kin of Totra!

Then he and his wife passed joyfully on over Family Cliff, unable to risk such another loss.

One day, Gautrek happened to be outside when he noticed the fine ox – the boy was seven years old at the time. It so happened that he stabbed the ox to death with a spear. Gilling was watching and said:

'The young boy has killed
that ox of mine,
a deadly sinister omen.
Never again
shall such treasure be mine,
no matter how old I grow.'

'This has really gone too far,' he added. And then he climbed up
Gillings Bluff and passed on over Family Cliff.

Now there were only two of them left, Snotra and her son Gautrek.
She made them both ready for a journey, and off they went all the way
to King Gauti who gave his son a good welcome.

So from then on Gautrek was brought up at his father's court. He
matured early in every way, and it only took him few years to reach full
manhood. Then it so happened that King Gauti fell ill and called his
friends around him.

'You've always proved obedient and loyal to me,' he said, 'but now it
looks as if this illness of mine is going to put an end to our friendship.
I've decided to hand over my authority to my son Gautrek, and with it
the title of King.'

His friends were all in favour of this, and after King Gauti's death
Gautrek was made King over Gotaland. He's mentioned in many of the
old sagas.

At this point we must shift our story north to Norway for a while
and tell you something about the provincial Kings who were ruling
there at the time and also about their progeny. After this, our story will
come back to King Gautrek of Gotaland and his sons.

This story is the same that's told in Sweden as well as in a good
many other lands.

3. STARKAD THE OLD

There was a King called Hunthjof who ruled over Hordaland. He was
the son of Frithjof the Brave and Ingibjorg the Fair. Hunthjof had
three sons: Herthjof, who later was King of Hordaland; Geirthjof, King
of the Uplands; and Frithjof, King of Telemark. All three brothers
were powerful kings and great warriors, but King Herthjof was more

shrewd and a better leader than either of the others. He spent a lot of
his time on viking expeditions, which earned him a great reputation.

At this time there was a king over Agder Province called Harald the
Agder-King. He was a powerful ruler, with a young, promising son
called Vikar.

There was a man called Storvirk, the son of Starkad the Ala-Warrior.
Starkad was a giant and had uncanny wisdom. He'd abducted a woman
called Alfhild, from Alfheim – King Alf's daughter. Then King Alf
called on Thor to bring his daughter back, so Thor killed Starkad and
carried Alfhild back to her father. She was going to have a child and
her son was the boy Storvirk whom we've already mentioned.

Storvirk was a fine-looking man, with black hair, and taller and
stronger than other men. He was a great viking, and joined the court
of King Harald of Agder Province, where he took charge of his defences. King Harald gave him Thruma Island in Agder and Storvirk
owned a farm there. He used to go on long viking expeditions, and at
other times he stayed with King Harald.

Storvirk abducted Unn, daughter of Earl Freki of Halogaland, and
after that he made his home on his island farm. They had a son called
Starkad.

Earl Freki's sons, Fjori and Fyri, made an attack on Storvirk one
night. They arrived unexpectedly with a force of men and burned
down the farm, killing Storvirk and their sister Unn and all the other
people who were in the house at the time. The attackers had not
wanted to risk opening the door in case Storvirk should escape. They
sailed away the same night and travelled north along the coast, but late
the following day they were overtaken by a sudden storm and ran on to
a submerged rock off Stad, where they were drowned with all hands.

Storvirk's son, Starkad, was very young when his father was killed,
and King Harald had him brought up at his court.* (1)

* At this point, the author begins to interpolate verses of a poem on the
life of Starkad. The points in the text where these verses occur are num-
bered 1–20 and a prose translation will be found against the appropriate
number on page 53. We have relegated all but the last two groups of verses
to the end of the saga, as they merely repeat the events described in the
prose narrative.

c

4. VENGEANCE

King Herthjof of Hordaland went out with an army, unexpectedly attacked King Harald one night, killed him treacherously, and took his son Vikar as hostage. King Herthjof conquered all of Harald's kingdom, made hostages of a good many more sons of important men and collected tributes throughout the whole country.

There was an important man in King Herthjof's army called Grani Horse-hair. He lived at Ask on Fenhring Island, off Hordaland. Grani took Starkad Storvirksson captive and brought him home with him to Fenhring. Starkhad was three years old at the time, and spent the next nine years at Fenhring with Grani Horse-hair. (2)

King Herthjof was a great warrior constantly at war, and there was always trouble in his own kingdom. He had warning beacons built on the mountains with watchmen in charge of them, so they could light the fires as soon as war broke out. Vikar and two other men looked after the beacons on Fenhring. At the first sign of enemy forces the nearest beacon was to be lit, and then the rest, one after another.

One morning shortly after he had taken charge of the beacon, Vikar went over to Ask to see his fosterbrother Starkad Storvirksson. Starkad was an exceptionally big man, but he was a layabout and slept among the ashes by the fire. He was twelve years old at the time. Vikar pulled him out of bed and gave him some weapons and clothes. When he took Starkad's measurements he was amazed to see how much he had grown since he had come to live at Ask. Later they went aboard Vikar's ship and sailed away. (3)

Starkad himself has said that although he was only twelve at the time he was already growing a beard. When Starkad had got to his feet, and Vikar had given him weapons and clothes, they went down to the ship and gathered a troop of men. He managed to get twelve, all of them warriors and duellers. (4)

With these men, Vikar marched against King Herthjof. As soon as the king heard of this attack he had his forces made ready. King Herthjof had a great house which was as strongly fortified as a castle or a town, and there he kept seventy warriors as well as all the farm-hands and other servants. The vikings wasted no time, for as soon as they arrived they started ramming the gates and doors and breaking down the door-posts, forcing the locks and bars inside them. The king's men fell back, the vikings were able to force their way into the house and a fierce skirmish began. (5)

King Herthjof had a number of excellent fighting men, so he was able to hold out for a long time, but since Vikar had a choice company of outstanding fighters, Herthjof's men had to give way. Vikar was always to the front of his men (6) and close by his side Starkad went hard against King Herthjof. Eventually they killed him. All Vikar's warriors fought like champions, killing a number of men and wounding many others. (7) So Vikar won the victory, and on King Herthjof's side thirty men were killed and a number fatally wounded, but Vikar didn't lose a single man.

After that Vikar took all the ships which had belonged to King Herthjof, and sailed east along the coast with as many men as he could muster. When he came to Agder he was joined by those who'd been his father's friends, so now he had a large body of men following him. Then he was made king over Agder and Jæderen Provinces, and soon he laid Hordaland under him, as well as Hardanger and all the other regions King Herthjof had ruled.

King Vikar soon became a powerful war leader. He used to go every summer on viking expeditions. Once he brought his forces east to Oslofjord and landed the army on the east coast, plundering as far as Gotaland and creating havoc there. When he reached Lake Væner he ran into King Sisar of Kiev, who was a great warrior and had a formidable army with him. The two kings, Vikar and Sisar, fought a hard battle there. Sisar made a sharp attack and killed a good number of Vikar's men. Starkad was there fighting on Vikar's side, and he moved up against Sisar. They fought for a long time, and neither could complain that the other was striking too feebly. Sisar hewed Starkad's shield to pieces with his sword and gave him two nasty head wounds and broke his collar bone. Starkad also got a wound on his side above the hip, (8) then another deep wound from Sisar's halberd on the opposite side. (9)

Starkad struck back at Sisar with his sword, slicing a piece off his side and wounding him badly in the leg below the knee. Finally he cut off Sisar's other leg at the ankle, and King Sisar fell down dead. (10)

There were a great many casualties in this battle, but Vikar won the victory, and the survivors of the Kiev forces were routed. After this victory King Vikar went back to his own kingdom.

5. HERTHJOF'S BROTHERS

King Vikar heard that King Geirthjof of the Uplands had gathered a large force, intending to attack Vikar and avenge the killing of his brother Herthjof. So Vikar ordered a general levy throughout his kingdom, and with this he marched against King Geirthjof of the Uplands. The battle between them was so fierce that they fought for seventeen days without a break. As it turned out King Geirthjof was killed, and Vikar won the victory and so he laid the Uplands and Telemark under him, since King Frithjof of Telemark happened to be away at the time. (11)

King Vikar left some of his men in charge of the kingdom he had won in the Uplands, and went back home to Agder; his power and his army had now become very great. He got himself a wife, and had two sons by her, the elder called Harald, and the younger Neri. Neri was the wisest of men, and every piece of advice he gave turned out for the best, but he was such a miser that he could never part with anything without immediately regretting it. (12) Earl Neri was a great warrior, but his meanness is a household word, and all the most niggardly men, the most reluctant to give anything to others, have been compared with him ever since.

When Frithjof heard that his two brothers had been killed he went to the Uplands and took back the kingdom Vikar had previously won. Then he sent word to Vikar, ordering him to pay tribute from his own land, or else look out for Frithjof's warriors. (13) As soon as Vikar got this message, he called a meeting and conferred with his councillors about how he ought to reply. They discussed the problem at great length. (14) Word was sent to King Frithjof that Vikar intended to defend his land. So Frithjof set off with his army to attack King Vikar.

There was a king called Olaf the Keen-eyed ruling over Næriki in

Sweden, a powerful ruler and a great warrior. Olaf ordered a general levy in his kingdom and with this force he went to support King Vikar. They had a huge army and set out to confront King Frithjof. Before the battle started they formed up in a wedge-shaped column. (15) There was some hard fighting, and Vikar's men advanced sturdily, since there were a good many famous warriors amongst them. First of all, there was Starkad Storvirksson, then Ulf and Erp and plenty of other great fighters and champions. King Vikar made a brave fight of it. Starkad was without a coat of mail, and waded through the enemy army hewing about him with both hands. (16) Vikar and his men kept this attack going fiercely until King Frithjof's army started breaking up and Frithjof was forced to ask King Vikar for mercy. (17)

It had been a very hard battle and most of King Frithjof's men were dead, so when he asked for peace Vikar ordered his army to stop fighting. Frithjof made a peace settlement with King Vikar, and King Olaf was to fix the terms. The final agreement was that King Frithjof should surrender his authority over the Uplands and Telemark. After that he went into exile.

King Vikar appointed his sons rulers of these territories. He made Harald king over Telemark and gave Neri the title of earl, and authority over the Uplands. Earl Neri became a friend of King Gautrek of Gotaland, and it's said in some books that King Gautrek gave him that part of Gotaland to rule over which was closest to the Uplands. It's also said that he was King Gautrek's earl and gave advice whenever the king was in need of it.

After this, King Vikar went back home to his own kingdom, and he and King Olaf parted great friends, as they remained for the rest of their lives. King Olaf went back home to Sweden.

6. THE FARMER'S BOY

There was a wealthy farmer called Rennir who lived on what came to be called Rennis Island, off Jæderen in Norway. He had been a great viking before he settled down on his farm. Rennir was married and had one son, called Ref.

When he was young Ref used to lie in the kitchen and eat twigs and tree bark. He was an exceptionally big man, but never bothered to wash the filth off his body, nor would he ever give anyone a helping hand. His father was a very thrifty man and took a very poor view of his son's shiftless behaviour. So Ref didn't earn his fame by any wisdom or bravery but rather by making himself the laughing stock of all his sturdy kinsmen. His father thought it unlikely that Ref would ever do anything worth while, as was expected at that time of other young men.

Rennir had one treasured possession which he valued more than anything else he owned, a big ox with very elegant horns Both horns had been incised and inlaid with gold and silver, and the point of the horn was also decorated with gold. There was a silver chain stretched between the horns, with three gold rings on it. This ox was the finest of its kind in the whole land, both for its size and magnificence. Rennir made such a fuss of this ox that it was never allowed to go about unattended.

Rennir took part in many of King Vikar's battles, and they were good friends.

7. THE GODS IN JUDGMENT

King Vikar became a great war leader and had with him a number of outstanding warriors, but Starkad was the most highly-regarded of them all and the one best loved by the king; he sat next to him on the high-seat, acted as his counsellor and was in charge of the defences. King Vikar had given him a good many striking gifts, one of them a gold bracelet weighing three marks. In return, Starkad gave the king Thruma Island, which King Harald had once given to Storvirk, Starkad's father. He was with King Vikar for fifteen years. (18)

King Vikar set out from Agder and sailed north to Hordaland with a large army. Then he ran into unfavourable winds and had to lie at anchor off a certain group of small islands. They tried by means of divination to find out when the wind would be favourable and were told that Odin expected a human sacrifice from the army, the victim to be chosen by lot. So they drew lots throughout the army and every time, King Vikar's lot came up. They were all very shaken by this, and it was decided that all their leading men should have a meeting the following day to consider the problem.

Then just about midnight, Grani Horse-hair woke up his foster-son Starkad and asked him to come along with him. They got a small boat and rowed over to another island. They walked through a wood until they came to a clearing where a large number of people were attending a meeting. There were eleven men sitting on chairs but a twelfth chair was empty. Starkad and his foster-father joined the assembly, and Grani Horse-hair seated himself on the twelfth chair. Everyone present greeted him by the name Odin, and he said that the judges would now have to decide on Starkad's fate.

Then Thor spoke up and said: 'Starkad's mother, Alfhild, preferred a brainy giant to Thor himself as the father of her son. So I ordain that Starkad himself shall have neither a son nor a daughter, and his family will end with him.'

Odin: 'I ordain that he shall live for three life spans.'

Thor: 'He shall commit a most foul deed in every one of them.'

Odin: 'I ordain that he shall have the best in weapons and clothing.'

Thor: 'I ordain that he shall have neither land nor estates.'

Odin: 'I give him this, that he shall have vast sums of money.'

Thor: 'I lay this curse on him, that he shall never be satisfied with what he has.'

Odin: 'I give him victory and fame in every battle.'

Thor: 'I lay this curse on him, that in every battle he shall be sorely wounded.'

Odin: 'I give him the art of poetry, so that he shall compose verses as fast as he can speak.'

Thor: 'He shall never remember afterwards what he composes.'

Odin: 'I ordain that he shall be most highly thought of by all the noblest people and the best.'

Thor: 'The common people shall hate him every one.'

Then the judges decreed that all that had been said should happen to Starkad. The assembly broke up, and Grani Horse-hair and Starkad went back to their boat.

'You should repay me well, my foster-son,' said Grani Horse-hair to Starkad, 'for all the help I've given you.'

'That I will,' said Starkad.

'Then you're to send King Vikar to me,' said Grani Horse-hair. 'I'll tell you how to go about it.'

Starkad agreed, and Grani Horse-hair gave him a spear which he said would seem to be only a reed stalk. Then they joined the rest of the army, just a little before daybreak.

In the morning the king's councillors held a meeting to discuss their plans. They agreed that they would have to hold a mock sacrifice, and Starkad told them how to set about it. There was a pine tree nearby and close to it a tall tree trunk. The pine tree had a slender branch just above the ground, but stretching up into the foliage. Just then the servants were making breakfast. A calf had been slaughtered and its entrails cleaned out. Starkad asked for the guts, then climbed up the trunk, bent down the slender branch and tied the calf guts around it.

'Your gallows is ready for you now, my lord,' he said to King Vikar, 'and it doesn't seem all that dangerous. So come over here and I'll put a noose round your neck.'

'If this contraption isn't any more dangerous than it looks,' said the king, 'then it can't do me much harm. But if things turn out otherwise, it's a matter for fate to decide.'

After that he climbed up the stump. Starkad put the noose round his neck and climbed down.

Next Starkad stabbed at the king with the reed stalk and said, 'Now I give you to Odin.'

Then Starkad let the branch loose. The reed stalk turned into a spear which went straight through the king, the tree stump slipped from under his feet, the calf guts turned into a strong withy, the branch shot up with the king into the foliage and there he died. Ever since, that place has been known as Vikarsholmar.

This business made Starkad hated by all the common people, and because of it he was first banished from Hordaland, and later had to flee from Norway east to Sweden. He stayed for a long time at Uppsala with the kings there, Eirik and Alrek (the sons of Agni Skjalf's-husband), and took part in viking expeditions with them. When Alrek asked Starkad what he could tell him about his kinsmen or himself, Starkad

composed the poem called *Vikar's Piece* in which he described how
King Vikar died.

'I fought with the greatest king of them all, and those were the
happiest years of my life. Then we went on our ill-starred and last trip
to Hordaland.

'It was then Thor ordained that I should become a traitor and suffer
other misfortunes. I was forced to commit wicked, infamous deeds.

'I was made to dedicate Vikar (the killer of Geirthjof) to the gods
high up in the tree. I thrust with a spear into the king's heart: no act of
mine has brought me such pain.'

'From there I wandered about unhappily and aimlessly – the people
of Hordaland hated me – a man with no gold and no songs, a kingless
man with his fill of sorrow.

'Then I drifted across to Sweden, to the Yngling Kings at Uppsala.
I shall long remember how indifferently I've been treated by those
royal retainers.'

It's quite obvious from Starkad's poem that he thought his killing of
Vikar the most wicked and hateful thing he ever did. We've never heard
any stories to indicate that Starkad ever returned to Norway again.

While Starkad was at Uppsala, twelve berserks were also there as
mercenaries. They were extremely aggressive and used to make fun of
him, particularly two brothers called Ulf and Otrygg. Starkad was very
taciturn and the berserks said he was a reborn giant as well as a
traitor; as it is said here:

'They placed me among the warriors – a white-browed mocked
old man. These men, unsparing in their cruelty, have made me their
laughing-stock and ridicule me.

'They claim they can see on me the Killer of Hergrim, the monstrous
scars which show the traces of eight arms torn off by Thor, north of the
cliffs.

'People laugh when they see me; the ugly jaws, the long snout-
shaped mouth, the wolf-grey hair and the tree-like arms, the bruised,
rough-skinned neck.'

When King Eirik and Alrek settled down, Starkad went on plundering expeditions with the ship that King Eirik had given him, manned
with Norwegians and Danes. He travelled widely, fought duels and
battles in many lands, and always won. And so Starkad is out of our
story.

King Alrek didn't live very long, and this is the way he died – his
brother, King Eirik, struck him dead with a bridle when they had gone
out to train their horses. After that King Eirek was the sole ruler of
Sweden for a long time, as will be told elsewhere in *Hrolf Gautreksson's
Saga*.

8. KING GAUTREK'S RULE

Now there are two series of events which have been taking place at the
same time, so we must go back to the point at which we broke off
earlier, when King Gautrek had become the ruler of Gotaland and
established himself as an outstanding leader and fighting man. Still, the
king felt it was a great flaw in his splendour that he had no wife, so he
decided to look out for one.

There was a king called Harald ruling over Wendland, a shrewd
man but not much of a fighter. He was married and had a daughter
called Alfhild, a fine-looking, well-mannered girl.

King Gautrek got ready for a journey and travelled to Wendland to
ask for King Harald's daughter. His proposal was well received, and
whatever was said, the outcome was this, that the princess was promised
to King Gautrek. So he brought her with him back to Gotaland and
celebrated their wedding. They hadn't been married long before Alfhild gave birth to a beautiful daughter. They chose a name for her and
called her Helga. She was a girl who matured early; she grew up with
her father, and was thought to be the finest match in all Gotaland.

King Gautrek had a number of very important men with him. One
of his friends was a great viking called Hrosskel. On one occasion King
Gautrek invited him to a feast, and when it was over, he gave Hrosskel
some excellent parting gifts: a grey stallion and four mares, silk-pale
and splendid. Hrosskel thanked the king for the presents, and they
parted the best of friends.

King Gautrek ruled his kingdom in peace for a number of years. Then his wife fell ill, and got no relief till she died. King Gautrek was deeply grieved by this, and had a burial mound raised over the queen. Her death affected him so much, he paid no attention to matters of state. Every day he used to sit on her mound and from there he would fly his hawk. This was his way of amusing himself and whiling away the time.

9. THE PRINCE AND THE PEASANT

Now we come back to Earl Neri, the ruler of the Uplands, whom we mentioned before. When he heard that his father, King Vikar, had been killed he arranged a meeting with his brother Harald, and there they discussed how they ought to divide their inheritance. They agreed that Harald, who was the elder, should take over all the kingdoms that King Vikar had ruled and have the king's title; but Earl Neri was to stay ruler of the Uplands and also get Telemark which up till then had been ruled by his brother Harald. The brothers parted on good terms. Earl Neri was so wise you could never find his equal, and all his plans turned out well, whatever the problem. He would never accept any gifts, for he was so mean he could never bring himself to give any in return.

One day the farmer Rennir, whom we've already mentioned, was passing through his kitchen and tripped over the feet of his son Ref.

'It's a terrible disgrace to have a son like you, you bring nothing but trouble,' said Rennir to his son. 'Well, you'd better get right out of my sight. And don't ever show your face here again, if you must act in this stupid way.'

'Since you're throwing me out,' said Ref, 'it's only fair I should take with me the thing you love and value most.'

'There's nothing I'm not willing to give for not having to see you again,' said Rennir, 'you're the laughing-stock of the family.'

Nothing more was said, but one fine day not long after, Ref rose to his feet and got ready to leave. He took the fine ox with him and led it down to the sea. Then he launched a large boat, intending to go over to the mainland. He didn't care whether or not the ox got a bit wet, so he tied it to the boat, then he sat down on the rowing bench and rowed over to the mainland. He was wearing a short cloak and breeches down to the ankles. When he had landed he set out with the ox behind him, travelling east through Jæderen and so by the usual route to the Uplands.

Ref journeyed on without a break until he arrived at Earl Neri's residence. The retainers told the earl that Ref, Rennir's idiot son, had arrived with the famous ox. The earl told them not to make fun of the boy. When Ref came up to the door of the hall where the earl usually sat, he told the doorkeeper to call the earl to come and talk with him.

'You're still the same fool as ever,' they said. 'The earl isn't in the habit of rushing out to talk with peasants.'

'You give him the message,' said Ref. 'He'll answer for himself.'

So they went inside to the earl and told him that Ref the Fool was asking for him to come out.

'Tell Ref I'll come and see him,' said the earl. 'You can never tell what may bring you luck.'

So the earl went outside, and Ref greeted him.

'What have you come here for?' asked the earl.

'My father's thrown me out,' said Ref. 'Here's an ox of mine I'd like you to have as a present.'

'Haven't you been told that I never accept gifts, as I don't like having to give any myself?' said the earl.

'I've heard you're so mean that no one can expect a gift in return for anything he's given you,' said Ref. 'But even so, I'd still like you to accept this ox as a gift. Maybe you could help me with your advice. Never mind the money.'

'Since you put it like that, I'll accept the ox,' said the earl. 'Come inside and stay the night.'

Ref let go of the ox and went into the house. The earl asked someone to bring Ref some clothes to make him look more decent, and when Ref had washed himself, he seemed a very handsome man. Ref settled there for a while.

The earl's hall was completely lined with overlapping shields, and not an empty space between them when they were all hanging. The earl took one of the shields, heavily inlaid with gold, and gave it to Ref.

Next day when the earl went to drink in the hall, he looked at the gap where the shield had hung, and said:

'The bright shield used to glitter
on the tapestried wall,
but now it gives me pain
to watch the empty space.
This is a fearful breach:
I'll soon lose all my wealth,
if others bring me gifts
and take my shields away.'

The earl had his high-seat turned round, for it upset him very much that the shield wasn't there any more.

When Ref realized this, he took the shield and went up to the earl.

'My lord,' he said, 'cheer up now, here's that shield you gave me. I'd like to give it back to you, for it's no use to me, I've no weapons to go with it.'

'Good luck to a generous man!' said the earl, 'now my hall will have its old splendour again, once the shield's back in its usual place. Here's a present I want to give you, and it may be you'll find it useful as long as you take my advice.'

The earl gave him a whetstone, 'but you'll probably think that this isn't a gift of very much value,' he said.

'I can't see how this can be much use to me,' said Ref.

'The fact is, I refuse to give food to any idler who hangs about doing nothing,' said the earl. 'Now I'm going to send you to King Gautrek, and you're to hand this whetstone to him.'

'This is the first time I've ever acted as an emissary between kings,' said Ref, 'and I can't see what possible use the king can have for this whetstone.'

'I'd hardly have a reputation for wisdom if I couldn't see further into the future than you,' said the earl. 'But this job won't in any way test your courage, since you're not even to talk to him. I've been told that the king often sits on the queen's burial mound, and flies his hawk from there. But as the day wears on, the hawk gets tired and then the king gropes round the chair to find something to throw at the bird. Now if it happens that the king can't find anything to throw at it, you're to put the whetstone into his hand. And if he gives you something in return you're to take it and then come back to me.'

So Ref set out as the earl had told him and travelled on till he arrived at the mound where King Gautrek was sitting. Everything turned out precisely as Earl Neri had said it would. The king threw all the objects he could lay his hands on at the hawk. Ref sat down behind the king's chair. Then he realized his turn had come, and when the king stretched his hand back, Ref put the whetstone into it, and the king hurled the stone at the hawk. The bird flew up as soon as the stone hit it. The king was so pleased with his success he didn't want his helper to go unrewarded, so without bothering to see who it was, he reached out behind him with a gold ring. Ref took it and went back to Earl Neri, who asked him how his trip had gone. Ref told him and showed him the ring.

'This is a valuable thing,' said the earl. 'It's a lot better to earn a thing like this than just sit around.'

Ref stayed there over the winter, and in the spring the earl asked him, 'What are you going to do now?'

'That shouldn't be difficult to decide,' said Ref. 'Now I can sell my ring for hard cash.'

'I'm going to take a hand in your affairs again,' said the earl. 'There's a king called Ælla who rules over England. You're to give him the ring, you won't lose by it. Come back to me in the autumn, I'll give you plenty of good food and advice even if I don't repay you for the ox any other way.'

'There's no need for you to bring that up,' said Ref.

Then he sailed over to England and went before King Ælla and greeted him courteously. On that occasion Ref was wearing fine clothes and weapons. The king wanted to know who this man was.

'I'm called Ref,' he said, 'and I'd like you to accept this gold ring as a present from me.'

Then he laid it on the table in front of the king.

The king looked at it. 'This is a great treasure,' he said. 'Who gave it you?'

'The ring was given me by King Gautrek,' said Ref.

'What had you given him?' said the king.

'A little whetstone,' said Ref.

'King Gautrek's a pretty generous man, to repay stone with gold,' said the king. 'I'm going to accept this ring, and invite you to stay with me.'

'Thank you, my lord, for your invitation. But I've decided to go back to my foster-father, Earl Neri.'

'You must stay here for a while,' said the king.

The king had a ship fitted out, and one day he asked Ref to come with him for a walk. 'Here's a ship I want to give you, with all the crew you need and a cargo of all the goods you'll find most useful,' said the king. 'Wherever you choose to go, I don't want you to be someone else's passenger any longer. But this isn't to be compared with King Gautrek's gift when he repaid you for the whetstone.'

'This is a most generous gift,' said Ref, and thanked the king for it with many well-chosen words and then made ready for the voyage.

The king said: 'Here are two little dogs I'd like to give you.'

These were exceptionally small and pretty, and Ref had never seen anything like them. They each wore a halter of gold with a gold clasp round their necks, and there were seven small rings on the chain that linked them. No one had seen any treasures quite like this before.

Then Ref put out and sailed on till he came to the land ruled by Earl Neri who went out to meet him and welcome him. 'Come with all your men and stay with me,' he said.

'I've money enough now to pay our own way,' said Ref.

'Good,' said the earl. 'But you mustn't spend your money on that. You're to eat at our table, that's not too much to pay for the ox.'

'The only thing that annoys me,' said Ref, 'is when you bring that up.'

So Ref spent the winter with the earl, and got on well with people, and plenty of men used to follow him around.

In the spring the earl said to Ref, 'What are you going to do now?'

'Wouldn't it be possible for me to go on a viking expedition or else go trading,' said Ref, 'now I've plenty of money?'

'That's true,' said the earl. 'But I'm still going to take a hand in your affairs. You're to go south to Denmark and see King Hrolf Kraki and give him the dogs. They're not the thing for ordinary people. You won't lose money by it if King Hrolf's willing to accept the gift.'

'I'll take your advice,' said Ref, 'though I've plenty of money already.'

10. KING HROLF

Ref made ready for a voyage and sailed over to Denmark. He went to see King Hrolf and greeted him, and the king asked him who he was. He said he was called Ref.

'Aren't you called Gift-Ref?' asked the king.

'It's true I've accepted gifts from people,' said Ref, 'and occasionally I've given presents to others.' Then he added: 'I'd like, Sir, to present you with these little dogs and their outfit.'

The king looked at them. 'These are very valuable,' he said. 'Who gave them to you?'

'King Ælla.'

'What had you given him?'

'A gold ring.'

'And who'd given you the gold ring?'

'King Gautrek.'

'And what had you given him?'

'A whetstone.'

'He's a remarkably generous man, King Gautrek, when he repays stones with gold,' said the king. 'I'd like to accept the dogs. You must stay with us.'

'I'm going back to Neri in the autumn,' said Ref.

'There's nothing to be done about it then,' said the king. So Ref stayed there for a while.

In the autumn Ref made his ship ready. Then the king said to him, 'I've decided how to repay you. Like the King of England, I'm going to present you with a ship, fully manned, and laden with the best cargo.'

'I can't thank you enough for this magnificent gift,' said Ref, and got ready to leave.

'Here are two valuable things I want to give you, Ref,' said the king, 'a helmet and a coat of mail.'

Ref took the gifts, both made of red gold, then he and King Hrolf parted good friends, and Ref went back to Earl Neri, this time in charge of two ships.

The earl welcomed him with open arms, and said his money had continued to increase . . . 'You'd better stay here with all your men over the winter. And even then I've only repaid you for the ox in a small way. But I'll never grudge you my good advice.'

'I'll accept your guidance in everything,' said Ref.

He stayed there over the winter enjoying fine hospitality, and getting a reputation as a famous man.

11. DECEPTION

In the spring Earl Neri asked Ref, 'What are you going to do this summer?'

'I'd like your advice, Sir,' said Ref. 'Now that I've plenty of money.'

'I think you're right about that but there's still one more trip I'd like you to make,' said the earl. 'There's a king called Olaf who's always plundering. He has eighty ships and lies out at sea, winter or warm summer. You're to go and give him the helmet and the coat of mail, and if he accepts the present, I expect he'll let you choose your own reward. Then you're to tell him that in return you want to command his forces for a fortnight and be free to take them wherever you like. The king has a councillor called Ref-Nose, who's a really evil character. It's doubtful which will be the stronger, your good luck or his magic, but you have to take the risk whatever happens. You're to bring all Olaf's forces here, and then maybe I can repay you for the ox.'

'You needn't keep on about that,' said Ref. And so they parted.

Ref put out to sea in search of King Olaf and found him with his fleet. He lay alongside the king's own ship, climbed aboard and presented himself. King Olaf asked him who he was, and Ref told him.

'Are you known as Gift-Ref?' asked the king.

'Some pretty eminent people have given me gifts,' admitted Ref, 'And I've always given them something too. Here are two valuable

D

things I'd like to present you with, a helmet and a coat of mail, both very fitting for a man like you.'

'Who gave you these precious things?' said King Olaf. 'I've never seen anything like them, nor even heard that such things existed, and yet I've been all over the world.'

'King Hrolf Kraki gave them to me,' said Ref.

'What had you given him?' asked the king.

'Two little dogs with gold halters that King Ælla had given me.'

'What had you given King Ælla?'

'A gold ring Gautrek had given me in return for a whetstone.'

'Some kings are remarkably open-handed,' said King Olaf, 'but King Gautrek outdoes them all in generosity. Should I accept these gifts, Ref-Nose, or should I reject them?'

'I wouldn't advise you to accept them,' said Ref-Nose, 'if you don't know how to repay them,' and with that he grabbed those precious objects and jumped overboard with them.

Ref realized that it would soon be the end of him if he failed to recover the things, so he went after him. There was a sharp skirmish between them, and the outcome was that Ref managed to get the coat of mail, but Ref-Nose held on to the helmet and dived with it down to the bottom of the sea where he went raving mad. By the time Ref managed to surface again, he was exhausted. Then someone said:

'It seems to me
Ref-Nose's advice
is a great deal worse
than Earl Neri's was.
King Gautrek the giver
of gold to Ref
didn't throw his money
into the sea.'

'You're a remarkable man,' said King Olaf.

'Well,' said Ref, 'I'd like you to accept this one treasure that's left.'

'I'm only too glad to accept it,' said King Olaf. 'I'm just as grateful to you as if I'd been given both treasures; and it was my mistake not to accept them straight away. But there's nothing surprising about that, it was an evil fellow's advice I was following. Now, I want you to choose your own reward.'

'I'd like to command your ships and forces for a fortnight,' said Ref, 'and take them wherever I please.'

'That's a queer choice,' said the king, 'but you're welcome to them.'

Then they sailed to Gotaland to meet Earl Neri. They landed there late in the day, and Ref sent messengers in secret to Earl Neri, asking him to come and see him. The earl went to see Ref, who told him all that had happened on his travels.

'Now the time's come, my friend, to put your good luck to the test,' said the earl. 'I want you to marry King Gautrek's daughter and form a family alliance with him.'

Ref said he'd trust in the earl's judgment.

'The next time we meet,' said the earl, 'whatever I say to you, don't show any surprise, and make sure you agree to anything I suggest.'

Then the earl rode off, and didn't stop until he came to King Gautrek's residence. It was just about midnight when the earl arrived and he told the king that an invincible army had invaded his country. 'These men intend to kill you and then lay the country under their rule.'

'Who's the leader of this army?'

'A man we'd never have believed would ignore my advice: my foster-son Ref.'

'Your word still carries a lot of weight with him,' said the king. 'Would it be wise to build up a force against him?'

'If you don't make peace with them,' said the earl, 'it seems pretty likely to me that they'll have caused a great deal of damage before you can muster your forces. I think it would be more sensible to make them a generous offer and find out whether you can reach a peaceful settlement. It seems to me any kingdom is on the verge of ruin when men like these start getting too close.'

'We've always been guided by your advice,' said the king.

'I'd like you, Sir, to hear what we have to say to each other,' said the earl.

The king said he'd do as the earl advised. Then they set out with a small number of men, and when they saw the enemy fleet, the king realized how many of them there were and how hard it would be to stand up against them.

The earl called out from the shore, shouting: 'Is it true that my foster-son is the leader of this army?'

'That's so,' said Ref.

'I'd never have thought, foster-son, that you'd attack either my territory or King Gautrek's. Is there anything we can offer to keep the peace?' asked the earl. 'I'm willing to do anything in my power to add to your reputation, and I'm sure King Gautrek will make the same promise on his own behalf. I'd like you to accept an honourable settlement from the king and then leave his kingdom in peace. I realize that you'll be very exacting in your demands, and that's only natural, seeing that your grandfather was a powerful earl and your father a great fighter.'

'I'll accept an honourable offer,' said Ref, 'if I get one.'

'I know you can't be bought off cheaply,' said the earl. 'I think I know the sort of thing you have in mind: you want to get my earldom, the one I've held under King Gautrek, and you'll be expecting the king to give you his daughter as well.'

'You've grasped the situation perfectly,' said Ref, 'and this is what I'll agree to as long as the king is willing.'

The earl turned to the king. 'It seems the wisest thing to accept this offer rather than risk our very lives against these killers. Anyway, it's not unlikely they'd first help themselves to your kingdom and then take your daughter captive,' he said. 'It would be perfectly honourable for you to marry your daughter to an earl's grandson. I'll help Ref with my advice if he's trusted with the government of your kingdom, assuming you'll go along with these proposals.'

'Earl Neri,' said King Gautrek, 'your advice has always been a great help to us, and I'm still willing to trust your foresight. Besides, I realize this army's too big a thing to handle.'

'My proposal is that Ref should be given a proper status so that he'll be able to strengthen your kingdom,' said the earl.

So this was agreed on and sealed with oaths, exactly as the earl had laid down the terms. Then King Gautrek went back home.

'You've given me plenty of support, King Olaf, and now you can go on your way, wherever you like,' said Ref.

'They're shrewd men who've had a hand in this affair of yours,' said King Olaf, and after that he sailed away.

And when the fleet had gone, King Gautrek said, 'I've been dealing with cunning men in this business, but I'll not break my oaths.'

The earl spoke to Ref: 'Now that you've only your own men left, you can see the value of my support. This advice was just the thing for you. It looks as though the ox has been paid off. All the same, I've been less generous than you deserve; for you gave me all you had, while I'm still left immensely rich.'

King Gautrek had a feast prepared, and there Ref married Helga, King Gautrek's daughter. The king also gave him the title of earl. Everybody thought Ref a very enterprising fellow; he was descended from men of rank, and his own father had been a great viking and champion. So Ref ruled his earldom, though he didn't live very long.

Earl Neri died suddenly, and there's nothing more to tell about him in this story. King Gautrek gave a funeral feast for him. By now the king himself was getting old and infirm. He'd won a great reputation for his generosity and bravery, but it's not said that he was a very profound thinker. However, he was well-liked and exceptionally open-handed, and was the most courteous of men.

And so we end Gift-Ref's Saga.

STARKAD'S VERSES (see p. 21)

1. Starkad himself refers to this: 'How young I was when my father perished with all his men in the fire. There he lies on Thruma Island, this great warrior, King Harald's retainer. Fjori and Fyri, Earl Freki's sons, destroyed their own sister's husband. They were my uncles, and brothers of Unn.'

2. This is what Starkad has said: 'Treacherously Herthjof treated his own lord, King Harald himself: he stole the life of Agder's ruler and put his sons into hard bondage. Grani Horse-hair abducted me to

Hordaland when I was three years old. So I grew up on Ask Island, for nine long years, without seeing my family.'

3. As Starkad himself has said: 'I grew in strength and my legs had lengthened like two poles. My head was a sight, for I used to sit in the ashes, taking no interest in anything. Then Vikar came from the beacon, where he'd been Herthjof's hostage, and walked into the room. He recognized me and urged me to get to my feet and speak to him. He measured me with his thumbs and hands, all my arms down to the wrists. I had hair growing on my cheek.'

4. In the words of Starkad: 'Then Vikar gathered a force, enlisting Sorkvir and Grettir, Hildigrim, Erp and Ulf, An and Skuma, Hroi and Hrotti, sons of Herbrand. Styr and Steinthor were there, from Stad in the north, and that old warrior Gunnolf Blaze. We were twelve together in all, and it would be hard to find a finer band of warriors.'

5. As Starkad said: 'When we arrived at the king's residence, we rammed the gates and hewed down the door frames. We broke the locks and drew our swords to face seventy royal warriors, besides a number of labourers, slaves and water-carriers.'

6. As Starkad said: 'How hard it was to keep up with Vikar who was always in the forefront of battle. We smashed their helmets and their heads as well, we sliced their mail-coats and broke their shields.'

7. As Starkad said: 'Vikar was fated to enhance his honour and to repay King Herthjof for his wicked deeds. We wounded the warriors and killed others. I was close by when the king was killed.'

8. As Starkad said: 'You were not with Vikar east at Lake Vanir early one day when we were fighting Sisar. That was a hard task, harder than you could imagine. He wounded me with his sharp-edged sword right through the shield and the helmet. He marked my skull and cut into my jaw as far as the teeth, and smashed my left collar bone.'

9. In the words of Starkad: 'The powerful warrior struck with his sword against my side above the hip; and at my other side he lunged with his cold-pointed halberd, deep into my body. You can still see the scars although the wounds are healed.'

10. As Starkad said: 'I took a slice off his side with my sharp sword, right across his body. So I used my weapon with all my strength, and did all I could.'

11. Starkad mentions also that the Battle of Uplands was Vikar's third battle: 'This courageous king now played his third game of war, and after that he won the Uplands when King Geirthjof had been despatched to Hell.'

12. As Starkad said: 'He had two outstanding sons, this famous king. The elder one was called Harald, later to rule Telemark. Earl Neri was said to be very mean with his money but shrewd in his advice and experienced in war. He was the sole ruler of the Uplands.'

13. As Starkad said: 'Frithjof sent an angry message to the wise king to find out which he would prefer: to pay tribute or suffer Frithjof's army.'

14. As Starkad said: 'We held long consultations and were not deceived. The army chose that the king should fight a battle.'

15. As Starkad said: 'King Olaf the Keen-eyed ruled his lands east in Sweden. He ordered out a levy, so his contingent formed a great part of the army.'

16. As this verse reports it: 'We advanced eagerly into the din of battle, King Vikar's men. Ulf and Erp were both to be seen there, and without any armour I fought with two hands.'

17. In the words of Starkad: 'Frithjof decided to ask for mercy, for Vikar was not going to yield and Starkad Storvirksson put all his strength into the fight.'

18. As Starkad himself had said: 'Vikar gave me foreign gold: the red bracelet which I wear on my arm, three marks in weight. But I gave him Thruma Island and my loyal support for fifteen years.'

Bosi and Herraud

1. HERRAUD'S FAMILY

There was a king called Hring who ruled over East Gotaland. His
father was King Gauti, the son of King Odin of Sweden. Odin had
travelled all the way from Asia, and all the noblest royal families in
Scandinavia are descended from him. Hring's half-brother on his
father's side was Gautrek the Generous, but his mother's family was
quite as outstanding.

Hring was married to a fine-looking, even-tempered woman called
Sylgja, the daughter of Earl Seafarer of the Smalands. She had two
brothers called Dayfarer and Nightfarer, both retainers of King Harald
Wartooth, who at that time ruled over Denmark and the greater part of
Scandinavia besides.

Hring and his queen had a son called Herraud. He was a tall handsome man, strong and talented, a man with very few equals. Everyone
was very fond of Herraud, except his own father who had no great
liking for him. As it happened, the king had another son, who was
illegitimate, and he was fonder of him than he was of Herraud. This
bastard son was called Purse and at this time he was a grown man, as
the king had begotten him when he was still young. The king granted
Purse large estates and made him his counsellor and tax collector.
Purse was in charge of levies and fee-estates, and he controlled the
king's revenues and expenses. Most people found him very grasping in
collecting the money and equally tight-fisted when he had to pay it out.
But he was loyal to the king and always had his interests at heart, and
so his name became a household word and people are called Pursers
who look after your interests and guard them with care.

To store the silver that was paid as dues to the king, Purse used
certain money-bags which have been known as purses ever since. But
what he collected over and above the rightful amount he used to preserve in smaller money bags which he called profit-purses. He used this
money for expenses, leaving the main tribute intact. Purse was not a
particularly popular man, but the king was very fond of him and let
him have his own way in everything.

2. BOSI'S FAMILY

There was a man called Thvari or Bryn-Thvari, who lived not far from
the king's residence. He had been a great viking in his younger years
and during his fighting career he had come up against an amazon,
Brynhild, the daughter of King Agnar of Noatown. They had set about
one another, and soon Brynhild was wounded and unable to carry on
fighting. Then Thvari took her into his care and also a great deal of
money with her. He saw to it that her wounds were healed completely,
but she remained bent and twisted for the rest of her life, and so she was
known as Stunt-Brynhild. Thvari made her his wife, and although she
wore a helmet and coat of mail at her wedding, their married life was a
happy one.

After that Thvari retired from viking life and settled down on a farm.
He and Brynhild had two sons. The elder, Smid, was not a tall man, but
exceptionally good-looking, very talented and extremely clever with
his hands. The younger son, Bosi, was a tall strong fellow, swarthy and
not so handsome. A cheerful, humorous man, he took after his mother
in personality and looks. Whatever he started, he would see it through,
and he never flinched, no matter whom he had to deal with. His mother
was very fond of him, and so he was nicknamed after her and called
Stunt-Bosi. He was a great joker both in what he said and did, so the
name suited him well.

There was an old woman called Busla, who had been Thvari's concubine, and fostered his sons for him. Busla was highly-skilled in
magic. She found Smid more amenable than his brother and taught him
a great deal. She offered to tutor Bosi in magic as well, but he said he
didn't want it written in his saga that he'd carried anything through by
magic instead of relying on his own manhood.

The king's son Herraud and the brothers were much of an age, and
they were also close friends. Bosi spent a lot of time at the royal court,
where he and Herraud were always together. Purse often complained
that Herraud used to give clothes to Bosi, since Bosi's clothes were
always getting torn. Bosi was considered a bit rough when he was
playing with the other boys, but no one dared complain about it
because of Herraud who always took his side. In the end, Purse

asked the king's men to give Bosi such a rough time that he'd stop playing.

3. BOSI JOINS HERRAUD'S EXPEDITION

On one occasion when the ball-game was getting a bit out of hand, the king's men started pushing Bosi around but he hit back and one of them dislocated an arm. The next day he broke someone's leg. On the third day two men went for him and a number of others got in his way. Then he knocked out the eye of one of them, and threw the other to the ground, breaking his neck. The king's men rushed for their weapons with the idea of killing Bosi, but Herraud stood by him with all the men he could get. They came very close to fighting, until the king turned up. At Purse's insistence the king made Bosi an outlaw, but Herraud helped him to escape so he wasn't caught.

A little later Herraud asked his father to give him some warships and sturdy men as he wanted to sail away and earn himself a reputation, if that was possible. The king put the matter to Purse, who answered that in his opinion the treasury would soon be empty if Herraud was to get all the outfit he wanted. The king said they would have to grant the request, and he got his own way. So preparations were made for Herraud's expedition and no cost was spared, for he was very particular about everything. He and Purse didn't see eye to eye over this.

Herraud set off with five ships, most of them old. He had brave men with him and a great deal of money, both gold and silver, and with this he sailed away from Gotaland south to Denmark.

One stormy day they saw a man standing on a cliff. He called out, asking them for a passage, but Herraud said he wasn't going out of his way for him, though he was welcome provided he could catch the ship. The man jumped off the cliff and landed on the tiller that jutted out from the helm, a leap of fifteen yards. Then everyone saw that it was Bosi. Herraud was delighted to see him and asked him to be the fore-castle-man on his own ship. From there they sailed to Saxony, plundering wherever they went, and getting plenty of money.

This went on for five years.

4. BOSI KILLS PURSE

Meanwhile, back in Gotaland, after Herraud had gone away, Purse inspected his father's treasury. When he saw that the coffers and bags were empty, he said the same thing over and over again. 'I remember the days,' he said, 'when this treasury was a happier sight.'

Then Purse set off to collect the royal tributes and taxes and was very exacting in most of his demands. He came to Thvari and ordered him to pay his levies, as others did, but Thvari answered that he was old enough to be exempt from the levy and said he wouldn't pay. Purse said that Thvari's duty was even greater than other men's, seeing it was his fault that Herraud had left the country. He wanted compensation as well for the men Bosi had injured, but Thvari said that anyone who played in a game had to look out for himself, and that he wasn't going to throw away his money on that account. This led to a heated argument between them and eventually Purse forced his way into Thvari's storeroom and took away two chests full of gold and plenty of other valuables, including weapons and clothes. After that they parted. Purse went back home with a great deal of money and told the king what had happened. The king told him it had been a mistake to rob Thvari as he would later find out to his cost, but Purse said that he wasn't in the least concerned.

Meanwhile, as Herraud and Bosi were getting ready to sail back home from their expedition, they heard about how Purse had robbed Thvari. Herraud decided then to try to set things right for Bosi and bring about a reconciliation between him and the king. They ran into a gale, so fierce that their ships were driven apart, and all the ships that Herraud had brought from home were lost. But with two other ships he managed to reach Elfar Skerries.

Bosi's ship was driven to Wendland. Shortly before, Purse had also arrived there with two ships from the Baltic countries where he'd bought some fine treasures for the king. When Bosi realized this, he told his men to arm themselves. Then he went to see Purse and asked him when he was going to pay back what he'd stolen from Thvari. Purse replied that Bosi was making a pretty impudent suggestion, since he'd already been outlawed by the king, and ought to count himself lucky if he lost no more than this. Then both sides seized their weapons and started fighting. The outcome was that Bosi killed Purse, and then spared the lives of all the rest, but he seized the ships and all that was on board.

As soon as he got a favourable wind, Bosi sailed over to Gotaland, where he found his foster-brother Herraud and told him what had happened. Herraud said that this wouldn't exactly endear him to the king. 'Why come to me when you've dealt me such a near blow?' he said.

'I knew that I'd never be able to escape you if you wanted revenge,' said Bosi, 'and anyway, you seemed to be the only person I could turn to.'

'It's true enough,' said Herraud, 'that Purse was no great loss, even though he was my kinsman. I'm going to see my father and try to reconcile you.'

Bosi said he didn't expect any great consideration from the king, but Herraud said they ought to try everything they could. So he went to see his father, and greeted him respectfully. His father received him coldly, as he'd already been told what had happened between Bosi and Purse.

Herraud said to his father, 'You've every right to demand compensation from my friend Bosi, he's made a great deal of mischief. He's killed your son Purse, though it wasn't without provocation. We'd like to make a settlement and offer you as much money as you want. Besides that we'll agree to pledge our loyal support and Bosi is willing to serve you in any way you like.'

The king replied angrily, 'Herraud, you're very determined to help this ruffian, but plenty of people would have thought it more your duty to avenge your brother and our disgrace.'

Herraud said, 'Purse was no great loss. I'm not even certain whether or not he was my brother, even though you were so fond of him. It seems to me you're showing me very little respect when you refuse to accept a reconciliation in spite of the plea I've made, and in my opinion, I'm offering a better man than Purse to take his place.'

The king had grown very angry and said, 'Your pleading on Bosi's behalf can only make matters worse. As soon as he's caught he'll be hanged on a higher gallows than any thief has ever had before.'

Herraud was angry too and replied, 'There are plenty of people who'll say you don't know where your honour lies. But since you're unwilling to show me any respect, you can take it that Bosi and I will share the same fate. I'll defend him as I would my own life, for as long as my courage lasts and till my dying day. Plenty of people will say that your bastard son was dearly bought if you decide to sacrifice us for his sake.'

Herraud was in a rage, and turned away. He didn't stop until he had found Bosi and told him what had happened between the king and himself.

5. BUSLA'S PRAYER

Hring had the alarm sounded to call his forces together, and then he went against the foster-brothers. The fighting began at once. The king had twice or three times as many men as they had, and though Herraud and Bosi fought bravely and killed a good many men, they were overpowered in the end, and shackled and thrown into the dungeon. The king was so furious he wanted to have them killed there and then but Herraud was very well-liked and everyone pleaded for his life. Then the booty was divided and the dead were buried. A number of people put it to the king that he ought to make peace with Herraud, and eventually Herraud was led before him. The king offered to spare his life, and many people spoke in favour of this, but Herraud refused the offer unless Bosi were spared as well. The king said that was out of the question. Herraud threatened to kill anyone who put Bosi to death, even the king himself. The king said it would serve Herraud right if he got the punishment he asked for. He was so angry no one could talk to him, and ordered Herraud to be taken back to the dungeon and the two men to be killed the following morning. The king was adamant, and it seemed to most people that the situation was quite hopeless.

That evening, Busla had a talk with her husband and asked him whether he wasn't going to offer some money for his son. Thvari answered that he'd no intention of throwing his money away, he knew only too well that he couldn't save the life of a doomed man soon to

die. Then he asked Busla what had become of her magic if she wasn't
going to give Bosi any help; but she said that she'd no intention of
competing with Thvari in meanness.

In the evening, Busla appeared in the king's bedroom and recited a
prayer which has been known as *Busla's Prayer* ever since. It has
become famous everywhere, and contains a good many wicked words
Christian mouths need never utter. This is how the prayer begins:

'Here lies Hring,
   Gotaland's king,
the most stubborn
   of mortal men.
You want to murder
   your son yourself:
an unheard of crime
   will make news far and wide.

Listen to Busla's
   prayer beginning;
soon it will echo
   throughout the world.
It will be a curse
   on all who hear it,
and cast into Hell
   the man of my prayer.

Demons shall run wild,
   dreadful things happen,
cliffs shall tremble,
   the world shall go mad;
weather shall worsen,
   dreadful things happen;
unless you, Hring,
   make peace with Herraud
and grant protection
   to my son Bosi.

E

Soon I shall come
close to your breast;
venomous snakes
shall gnaw at your heart;
your ears go deaf,
your eyes turn inwards;
unless you have mercy
on my son Bosi,
and give up your hatred
of Herraud too.

When you go sailing,
the rigging shall break,
and the hooks on your rudder
shall snap asunder,
the sails shall tear
and be swamped by the sea,
the braces shall break;
unless you give up
your hatred of Herraud,
and plead with Bosi
to come to terms.

When you go riding,
your bridle shall break,
your horse go lame
and waste away;
all of your paths
shall lead you straight
to the clutch of monsters;
unless you have mercy
on my son Bosi,
and give up your hatred
of Herraud too.

Your bed shall feel
like burning straw,
and your high-seat
like the swollen sea;
Yet shall you fare worse
when you want to play
the man's game with women
for you won't know the way.
Do you want any more?'

'Shut your mouth, you filthy creature,' said the king, 'and get out of
here, or I'll have you tortured for your curses.'

'Now that we've met,' said Busla, 'it's not likely that we'll part till I
have what I came for.'

The king wanted to stand up, but he was stuck fast to the bed, and
none of his servants could be roused from their sleep. Then Busla
recited the second part of her prayer, but I'd better not write it here, as
people repeat it only at their peril. If it's not written down, the prayer is
less likely to be repeated. All the same, this is the beginning:

Trolls and elves
and sorceresses,
goblins and giants
shall burn your halls;
frost-giants shall fright you
and stallions ride you,
straws shall sting you,
storms drive you mad;
may you ever be damned,
unless you do what I want.'

When the second part was over, the king said to Busla, 'Rather than
have you cursing me any longer, I'm going to let Herraud live. But
Bosi must leave the country and if ever I lay hands on him he'll be
killed.'

'In that case, I'll have to deal with you further,' said Busla.

Then she started reciting the so-called *Syrpa Verses* which contain the most powerful magic, and which nobody is allowed to sing after sun-set. This stanza comes near the end:

'Here are the names
of six strangers,
and you must now
decipher them.
If you should fail
to solve this riddle
in such a way
as will satisfy me
the dogs of Hell
shall tear you to death,
and your soul sink
down to damnation.

ᚱ.ᚠ.ᚦ.ᚴ.ᚢ.ᚿ||||||| ᛏᛏᛏᛏᛏᛏ:ᛁᛁᛁᛁᛁᛁ:||||||:ᚱᚱᚱᚱᚱᚱ:*

'Now you'd better interpret these names correctly or else do what I want: otherwise all my worst curses will bite you.'

When Busla had completed her prayer, the king had no idea how he ought to react to her demands. 'What do you want, then?' he asked.

'You're to send Bosi and Herraud on a dangerous mission,' said Busla, '– who knows how it will end – and they're to be responsible for their own safety.'

The king told her to go away but she refused to leave until he'd given his solemn word to carry out his promises to her; and after that, Busla's prayer could do him no harm.

Then the old hag went away.

6. BOSI'S MISSION

Early next morning the king got up and had the alarm sounded to call people to a meeting, and then Herraud and Bosi were led before the

* See Note on the Translations, p. 21.

gathering. The king asked his councillors what should be done with the two men, and most of them pleaded with him to spare Herraud.

Then the king spoke to his son. 'You don't seem inclined to show me much respect,' he said, 'but in spite of that I'm going to do as my friends ask me: I'm going to spare Bosi's life. He's to leave this country and not come back until he brings me a vulture's egg, inscribed all over with gold letters, and then we'll be reconciled. If not, everyone can take it he's a coward. Herraud is free to go wherever he wants to, either with Bosi or on any other course he likes. I only want him to stay away from me after what's happened.'

After that the two men were set free. They went to Thvari and stopped with him over the winter. In the spring they got ready for a voyage with one ship and a crew of twenty-four. By and large, they let themselves be guided by Busla's advice. And so they set off and sailed east across the Baltic, and when they came to Permia they brought their ships in under cover of a certain thickly-forested wilderness.

7. A NIGHT IN THE WOOD

At that time the ruler of Permia was King Harek, a married man with two sons, Hrærek and Siggeir. They were great fighters, serving at the court of King Godmund of Glasir Plains, and they were also in charge of the country's defences. King Harek had a daughter called Edda, a beautiful woman and in most matters unusually talented.

Now we must return to the foster-brothers, who were lying off Vina Forest in Permia where they'd set up a tent ashore in a remote and desolate spot.

One morning Bosi told his men he was going ashore with Herraud to explore the forest and see what they could find. 'You're to wait a month for us here, and if we're not back by then, you can sail wherever you like.' Their men weren't too happy about this, but there was nothing they could do about it.

The foster-brothers made their way into the wood. They had nothing to eat except what they could catch by shooting deer and birds; sometimes their only food was berries and the sap of the trees, and their clothes were badly torn by the branches.

One day they came upon a cottage. An old man was standing outside it splitting firewood, and he greeted them and asked them their names. They told him who they were and asked him his name, and he said he was called Hoketil. Then he told them they were welcome to stay the night if they wanted to, so they accepted his offer. The old man showed them to the living-room, and very few people were to be seen there. The woman of the house was getting on in years, but there was an attractive young daughter. The girl pulled off their wet clothes and gave them dry things instead, then brought a basin so they could wash their hands. The table was laid, and the young woman served them with excellent ale. Bosi kept eyeing her suggestively and touching her foot with his toe, and she did the same to him.

In the evening they were shown to a comfortable bed. The farmer slept in a bed-closet, his daughter in the middle of the room and the foster-brothers in a bed under the gable beside the door. When the people were asleep, Bosi got up, went over to the young woman's bed and lifted the beclothes off her. She asked who was there, and Bosi told her.

'What have you come for?' she asked.

'I wasn't comfortable enough in my bed as things were,' he said, and added that he'd like to get under the bedclothes with her.

'What do you want to do here?' she said.

'I want to temper my warrior,' said Bosi.

'What sort of warrior's that?' she asked.

'He's still very young and he's never been steeled,' he said, 'but a warrior ought to be hardened early on in life.'

He gave her a gold ring and got into bed beside her. She asked him where the warrior was, and he told her to feel between his legs. But she pulled her hand back and said the devil could take that warrior of his and asked why he was carrying a monster like that on him, as hard as a tree. He told her the warrior would soften in the dark hole, and then she said he could do anything he wanted. So now he set the warrior between her legs. The path before him was rather narrow, and yet he managed to complete his mission.

After that they lay quiet for a while, as long as they pleased, and then the girl asked him if the tempering of the warrior had been a complete

success. Bosi asked her in turn whether she felt like tempering him
again, and she said she'd be only too pleased as long as he felt the need
for it.

It's not recorded how often they played the game that night, but it's
known that Bosi asked her, 'Have you any idea where I can find a
vulture's egg inscribed with gold letters? My foster-brother and I have
been sent to find out.'

She said the very least she could do in payment for the gold ring and
a good night's entertainment was to tell him all he wanted to know.

'But who's so angry with you that he wants you dead, sending you
on such a dangerous mission?'

'Evil motives aren't the only motives, and no one can get much of a
reputation without some effort,' said Bosi. 'There are plenty of affairs
full of danger to start with, that bring you good luck in the end.'

8. THE VULTURE'S EGG

'In this forest,' said the girl, 'there's a large temple belonging to King
Harek, the ruler of Permia. The god worshipped there is called Jomali,
and a great quantity of gold and jewels is to be found there, too. The
king's mother, Kolfrosta, is in charge of the temple. She's so powerful
with her witchcraft, nothing could ever take her by surprise. By her
sorcery she's been able to predict that she won't live out the month, so
she's travelled by magic east to Glasir Plains and carried off King
Godmund's sister, Hleid, whom she means to take her place as the
priestess of the temple. But that would be a loss indeed – Hleid's one of
the most beautiful and well-bred of women – so it would be all for the
best if it could be prevented.'

'What's the main snag about the temple?' Bosi asked.

She said, 'There's an enormous vulture there, so savage it exter-
minates everything that comes anywhere near it. The vulture stares at
the door and sees everything that comes inside. There's not a man alive
has a chance of survival if the vulture's claws and venom come anywhere near him. Underneath this vulture lies the egg you've been sent
after.

'There's also a slave in the temple, who looks after the priestess's food – she eats a two-year-old heifer at every meal. And there's a bewitched and enchanted bull in the temple, shackled with iron chains. The bull's supposed to mount the heifer, poisoning her flesh, and then all those who taste it go crazy. The heifer's to be cooked for Hleid, and then she'll turn into a monster like the priestess.

'As things are, I don't think it's very likely you'll be able to beat these devils, considering all the sorcery you're up against.'

Bosi thanked her for telling him all this and repaid her handsomely with yet another round of good entertainment. They were both very pleased with themselves, and slept till dawn. In the morning, he went over to Herraud and repeated what he'd been told. They stayed on for another three nights, and then the farmer's daughter told them the way they should go to the temple. She wished them luck, and they set out on their journey.

Early one morning they saw a tall man in a grey cloak leading a cow. They realized this must be the slave, so they went for him. Bosi struck him a heavy blow with a club, and that was the end of him. Then they killed the heifer and skinned her, and stuffed the hide with moss and heather. Herraud put on the slave's cloak and dragged the heifer's skin behind him. Bosi threw his cloak over the slave's body and carried him on his back. When they came in sight of the temple, Bosi took his spear and drove it into the slave's backside and up through the body so it jutted out of the shoulder. They walked up to the temple and, wearing the slave's clothes, Herraud went inside.

The priestess was asleep. Herraud led the heifer into the stall and then untied the bull, and the bull mounted the heifer at once. But the moss-filled hide collapsed on impact, so that the bull fell forward against the stone wall, breaking both its horns. Herraud grabbed the bull by the ears and the jaw, and gave the neck such a violent twist that it broke.

At that moment the priestess woke up and jumped to her feet, as Bosi walked into the temple carrying the slave over his head by the spear. The vulture wasted no time and dived down from the nest, intending to make a meal of this intruder. But it only swallowed the upper part of the corpse, and Bosi gave the spear a hard push so that it went straight through the vulture's throat and into the heart. The vulture set its claws hard against the slave's buttocks and struck its wing tips against Bosi's ears, knocking him unconscious. Then the vulture crashed down on top of him, ferocious in its death-throes.

Herraud made for the priestess, and there was a hard struggle between them, as she wore her nails cut jagged and tore his flesh down to the bone. The tussle took them to the spot where Bosi was lying, the floor around him covered with blood. The priestess slipped in the vulture's blood and fell flat on her back, and so the struggle continued as fierce as ever, with Herraud sometimes on top of her and sometimes underneath.

Then Bosi came to, got hold of the bull's head and hit the old hag hard on the nose with it. Herraud tore one of her arms off at the shoulder, and after that her spirit began to weaken. Even so, her final death throes caused an earthquake.

After that they went through the temple and searched it thoroughly. In the vulture's nest they found the egg, all covered with letters in gold. They found so much gold there they had more than enough to carry. Then they came to the altar where Jomali was sitting, and from him they took a gold crown set with twelve precious stones; also a necklace worth three hundred gold marks; and off his knees they took a silver cup filled with red gold and so big that four men couldn't drink it up. The fine canopy that was hung over the god was more valuable than three cargoes of the richest merchantman that sails the Mediterranean; and all this they took for themselves.

In the temple they found a secret side room with a stone door, securely locked. It took them the whole day to break it open and get inside. There they saw a woman sitting on a chair – never had they seen such a beautiful woman! Her hair was tied to the chair posts, and was as fair as polished straw or threads of gold. An iron chain, firmly locked, lay round her waist, and she was in tears.

When she saw the men, she asked them what had been causing all the uproar that morning. 'Do you care so little for your lives that you're willing to put yourselves into the power of demons? The masters of this place will kill you the moment they see you here.'

They said there'd be plenty of time to talk about that later. Then they asked her what her name was, and why she was being treated so badly.

She said her name was Hleid and that she was the sister of King Godmund of Glasir Plains in the east.

'The ogress in charge here got hold of me by magic and wants me to become priestess here when she's dead and take over the sacrifice in the temple. But I'd rather be burnt alive.'

'You'd be good to the man who helped you escape from here?' said Herraud. She said she didn't think anyone could possibly manage that.

'Will you marry me if I take you away?' asked Herraud.

'I don't know a man on earth so loathsome I'd not prefer being married to him rather than worshipped in this temple. What's your name?'

'I'm called Herraud,' he said, 'and my father is King Hring of East Gotaland. You needn't worry any more about the priestess. Bosi and I have already given her a good send-off. But you'll realize that I feel entitled to some reward from you if I get you out of this place.'

'I've nothing to offer but myself,' she said, 'that is, if my family will let me.'

'I don't intend to ask them,' said Herraud, 'and I won't have any more evasion, since it seems to me that I'm every bit as good as you. So whatever you decide, I'll set you free.'

'Of all the men I've ever set eyes on, there's no one I'd rather have than you,' she said.

Then they set her free. Herraud asked what she would prefer, to travel home with them and become his wife; or else to be sent east to her brother, never to see Herraud again. She chose to go with him, and so they pledged themselves to each other.

They carried the gold and treasures out of the temple and then set fire to the building and burned it to ashes so that there was nothing else to be seen there. After that they set off with all that they'd taken and didn't break their journey till they reached Hoketil's house. Nor did they stay there very long, but gave him a great deal of money, and then carried the gold and treasures on a number of horses down to the ship.

Their men were delighted to see them.

9. THE BATTLE OF BROW PLAINS

They sailed away from Permia as soon as the wind was in their favour, and there's nothing to tell of their voyage until they arrived back home in Gotaland, after being away two years. They went before the king, and Bosi delivered the egg. The shell was cracked, and even the broken piece was worth ten gold marks. The king used the shell as a loving-cup. Bosi also gave him the silver cup that he'd taken from Jomali and now they were completely reconciled.

About this time the queen's brothers, Dayfarer and Nightfarer, came to the royal court. They had been sent by King Harald War-tooth to ask for support, as a time had been set for the Battle of Brow Plains. This battle was the greatest ever fought in Scandinavia, and is described in the *Saga of Sigurd Hring*, the father of Ragnar Hairy-Breeks.

Meanwhile, Hring asked Herraud to go in his place, and offered to look after the bride. He also said that he and Herraud should be fully reconciled over everything that had happened between them. Herraud did as his father asked. He and Bosi joined the brothers with five hundred men and went to King Harald. In this battle King Harald and one hundred and fifteen other kings were killed, as it says in his Saga, and a good many great champions as well, even greater men than the kings themselves. Both Dayfarer and Nightfarer were killed. Herraud and Bosi were wounded but managed to come out of the battle alive.

Meanwhile in Gotaland, great changes had taken place while they were away, as will soon be told.

10. THE DEATH OF HRING

Since it's not feasible to tell more than one story at a time, we'd now better explain what had happened earlier on. We begin at the point where King Godmund's sister, Hleid, had vanished from Glasir Plains. As soon as the king realized she had disappeared, he had a search made for her by sea and land, but no one could find any trace of her. The two brothers, Hrærek and Siggeir, were staying with the king at the time. The king asked Siggeir to take charge of the search for Hleid, and as a reward he was to win her as his wife. Siggeir said that in his opinion Hleid would be very hard to trace, unless the priestess in Permia knew where she was. The brothers got ready to sail away with five ships. When they reached Permia, they found King Harek and told him about their mission. He advised them to go to the temple, and said that if neither the god Jomali nor the priestess knew Hleid's whereabouts, there wasn't much hope of finding her. The brothers went to the temple and saw nothing but a vast heap of ashes, with not a sign of anything that should have been there.

The brothers scoured the forest until they came upon Hoketil's house. They asked if he or his household had any idea who could have destroyed the temple. The old man said he didn't know, but he mentioned that two men from Gotaland had been lying at anchor for a long time off Vina Forest, one called Herraud and the other, Bosi. In his opinion they were the most likely men to have done such an extraordinary thing. The farmer's daughter said she had seen these men on their way to the ship, bringing King Godmund's sister with them, Hleid of Glasir Plains. They had told the girl that anyone who wanted to see Hleid should come to them.

When the brothers realized what had happened, they told the king about it. Then they gathered forces all over Permia and with twenty-three ships they sailed to Gotaland. They arrived there about the time of the Battle of Brow Plains where the foster brothers were fighting, so Hring had only a small force with him. Hrærek and Siggeir told him either to fight or else hand over Hleid to them. The king chose rather to fight, but the matter was soon settled as Hring and the greater part of his army were killed.

Then the brothers took the girl, stole all the money they could and sailed back without stopping to Glasir Plains. King Godmund was delighted to get his sister back and thanked them generously for their mission, which was considered a great success. Siggeir made a proposal of marriage to Hleid, but she was far from willing and said it would be more fitting if she were to marry the man who had saved her from the monsters.

The king said that Siggeir fully deserved to have her and added that he himself was the one to settle her marriage. 'And no foreign princes are going to have you, even if you won't accept my decision.' So she had to do as the king wished.

Now we'd better let them get on with their wedding, since they are looking forward to it so much. Still, it may happen yet that the feast won't go without a hitch.

11. BOSI'S ADVENTURES

Now we'd better explain that Herraud and Bosi arrived home in Gotaland a fortnight after Siggeir and his men had sailed away. Their return was a great disappointment to them, but they took stock of the situation and then Bosi went to his father to ask for advice. Thvari said there was no time to gather a whole army and the only way of rescuing Hleid was by means of carefully-laid plans and swift action. So the outcome was that they got ready a single ship with thirty men aboard. It was decided that Smid should go with them and be in charge of the expedition. Thvari gave them a lot of sound advice, and so did Busla.

They set off as soon as they were ready. Smid always had a favourable wind whenever he was at the helm, so their voyage was much faster than anyone might have expected. Soon the brothers had reached Glasir Plains in the east. They cast anchor off a certain thickly-wooded coast, and Smid threw a helmet of invisibility over the ship.

Herraud and Bosi went ashore and came to a small well-kept cottage. An old man was living there with his wife, and they had an attractive and well-informed daughter. The peasant gave them an invitation to stay the night, which they accepted. The cottage was quite comfortable, and the hospitality good. The table was laid, and the guests were served with excellent beer. The master of the house was silent and reserved, but his daughter, the most sociable member of the household, was the one who served the guests. Bosi was in a good humour and flirted with her a little, and she did the same to him.

In the evening they were shown to their beds, but as soon as the light had been put out, Bosi went over to the girl and lifted the bed-clothes off her. She asked who was there, and Bosi told her.

'What do you want?' she asked.

'I'd like to water my colt at your wine-spring,' he said.

'Do you think you can manage it, my man?' she asked. 'He's hardly used to a well like mine.'

'I'll lead him right on to the edge, and then push him in if there's no other way to make him drink,' said Bosi.

'Where is your colt, sweetheart?' she asked.

'Between my legs, love,' he said. 'You can touch him, but do it gently, because he's very shy.'

She took hold of the prick, and stroked it and said, 'He seems a lively colt, though his neck is much too straight.'

'His head isn't all that well set,' agreed Bosi, 'but he can curve his neck much better after he's had a drink.'

'Well, it's all up to you now,' she said.

'Lie as open as you can and keep calm,' said Bosi.

Then he watered his colt generously, completely immersing him. This pleased the girl immensely, and she was hardly able to speak. 'Are you sure you're not drowning the colt?' she asked.

'He has to be given as much as he can possibly take,' said Bosi, 'he often gives me a lot of trouble when he isn't allowed to drink to his satisfaction.'

Bosi kept this going for as long as he felt like it, and then he took a rest. The girl was wondering where all the fluid between her legs had come from, for the whole bed was lathering under her.

She said, 'Could it be your colt's drunk more than was good for him and then vomited up more than he's drunk?'

'Something seems to be wrong with him, he's as soft as a lung,' said Bosi.

'He's probably ale-sick,' she said, 'like any other drunkard.'

'I dare say,' he said.

They amused themselves to their satisfaction, the girl being now under him and now on top. She said she'd never ridden a more slow-paced colt than this one.

After a good many entertaining turns, she asked him who he was. He told her and in turn asked her what was the latest news in the land. The very latest news, she replied, was that the brothers Siggeir and Hrærek had got back the King's sister, Hleid, from Gotaland and killed Hring.

'And this has got them such a reputation that no one here in the east can measure up to them. The king has promised his sister Hleid to Siggeir against her wishes, and the wedding is to be in three days' time. The brothers are very much on their guard, they've spies on every road and at every harbour. It's impossible to take them by surprise. They're expecting Herraud and Bosi to come at any time to fetch Hleid.

'The king has had a hall built, so enormous there's a hundred doors in it, with the same distance between each of them, and a hundred men can sit in every space. There are two watchmen at every door, and no one is allowed to pass through unless he's been vouched for by one of the doorkeepers. Those who aren't recognized at any of the doors are to be kept in the dungeons until it's known who they are. There's a raised bed standing in the middle of the floor of the hall, with four steps leading up to it. The bride and bridegroom are to lie there, and all the retainers will be keeping watch round the bed, so it's impossible to catch them unawares.'

'Which of the retainers is the King's favourite?' asked Bosi.

'He's called Sigurd,' she said, 'the king's counsellor. He's a remarkable musician, there's nobody to compare with him anywhere, particularly at playing the harp. Just now Sigurd's visiting his concubine, she's a peasant's daughter living near the forest. She makes him clothes while he tunes his instruments.'

After that they dropped the subject and for the rest of the night they slept.

12. A WEDDING FEAST

Early in the morning Bosi went back to Herraud and told him what he'd learnt during the night. Then they got ready to leave, and Bosi gave the young woman a gold ring. They followed her instructions about which way they ought to go, until they came in sight of the farm where Sigurd was staying. Then they saw him making for the royal palace with a servant. The foster brothers stepped forward into their path. Bosi drove his spear through Sigurd, and Herraud strangled the servant. Afterwards, Bosi flayed the bodies. Then they went back to the ship and told Smid what they had done, and between them they settled their plans. Smid put Sigurd's clothes and the skin of his face on Bosi, and wore the other mask and the servant's outfit himself.

Then they told Herraud what he had to do and walked up to the palace. They came up to the door where King Godmund was waiting, and he thought this was Sigurd, so he welcomed him and led him into the palace. 'Sigurd' took charge of the royal coffers, and of the ale-supplies and wine-cellars, too. It was he who decided what ale should be served first, and told the cup-bearers how generously they were to serve the drinks. He said it was most important that the guests should get as drunk as possible on the first night of the feast, since in that way they would stay drunk much longer.

Then all the important guests were shown to their seats, and the bride was escorted into the palace and led to her bench with a large company of elegant young women.

King Godmund sat on the high-seat. Beside him sat the bridegroom, with Hrærek in attendance on him. It isn't said how the other noble-men were placed, but this much is known, that 'Sigurd' played the harp before the bride and her maidens. When the toasts were being served, 'Sigurd' played so well, everyone remarked that he had no equal, but he said this was only the beginning. The king told him to put all he could into his efforts. When the memorial cup consecrated to Thor was carried into the hall, 'Sigurd' changed the tune. Then every-thing loose began to move – knives, plates and anything else which no one was holding on to – and lots of people jumped up from their seats and danced on the floor. This went on for quite a long time.

Next came the toast dedicated to all the gods. 'Sigurd' changed the tune again, and this time he played so loud, the music rang through the entire palace. All the people inside jumped to their feet, except the king and the bridal couple. For a long time all the guests were shuffling about and so was everything else inside the hall. This went on for quite a long time.

The king asked whether 'Sigurd' knew any more tunes. He answered that there were still a few less important ones and advised everybody to take a rest for a while. The guests sat down and carried on with their drinking. Then he played the tunes of the *Ogress*, the *Dreamer* and the

Warrior, and after that it was time for Odin's toast to be drunk. Then 'Sigurd' opened the harp. It was heavily inlaid with gold, and so big that a man could stand upright inside it. From inside he took a pair of white gloves, gold-embroidered, and played the *Coif-Thrower*. Then all the coifs were blown off the ladies' heads, and danced above the cross-beams in the hall. All the men and women jumped to their feet, and not a single thing remained still in its place.

When Odin's toast had been drunk, there was only one more left, the toast dedicated to Freyja. Then 'Sigurd' started plucking the one string that lies across the other strings, and told the king to get ready for the tune called *Powerful*. The king was so startled at this tune that he jumped to his feet and the bride and the bridegroom too, and nobody danced more vigorously than they did. This went on for quite a long time. Now Smid took the bride by the hand and led her a lively dance, and when he got the chance, he picked up the table service and bundled it into the bridal sheets.

Now we come back to Herraud, who told his men to stove in all the ships along the coast, making them unseaworthy. He sent some others up to the town to collect the gold and jewels that Smid had put ready for them to carry down to the sea. By now it was growing very dark. Some of the men were on the roof of the palace, watching what was happening inside and hauling up through the skylight what had been thrown into the sheets. Others carried this down to the ship, which had been pointed out to sea.

13. ABDUCTION

The next thing to happen was this. While the people in the palace were having their fling, a stranger walked inside, a tall, handsome man wearing a red scarlet tunic, with a silver belt round his waist and a gold band on his forehead. He was unarmed and started dancing like the others. When he came before the high-seat, he raised his fist and punched the king so hard on the nose that three teeth shot out of his mouth. The king's nose and mouth began to pour with blood and he fell unconscious on to the floor.

'Sigurd' saw what had happened, and threw the harp into the bed.

F

Then he struck at the stranger with both fists between the shoulder-blades. The man turned away, with 'Sigurd' after him. A good many followed, while others were attending to the king. Now 'Sigurd' took the bride by the hand, led her up to the bed and locked her inside the harp, and the men on the roof hauled her and Smid up through the skylight. After that they hurried down to the ship and went on board. The man who had hit the king was already there before them. 'Sigurd' stepped aboard as soon as he arrived, but Siggeir was right behind him with a sword in his hand. Then 'Sigurd' turned round to face him and pushed him into the sea. Siggeir's men had to fish him out of the water, more dead than alive.

Smid cut the moorings, and the crew set sail. They tried to reach open water as fast as they could by rowing and sailing at the same time. Hrærek rushed down to the sea with a number of other men to launch their ships, but the coal-black sea poured in, and they had to make their way back to the shore. There was in fact nothing much they could do about it, as all the men were helplessly drunk.

The king was very shaky when he came to. He was offered some food, but he was still too weak to take any. The festivities had turned sour and sorry. Still, when the king had recovered, they made their plans. They decided not to disband but get themselves ready as quickly as they could to chase after the foster-brothers.

While they are busy getting ready, we must take up the story of the others. They sailed on their way till they came to the point where one route lies to Gotaland and the other to Permia. Then Bosi told Herraud to sail on to Gotaland and said he himself had some business in Permia.

Herraud said he was not going to leave him. 'What's your business there anyway?' he asked.

Bosi said this would become clear later. Smid offered to wait for them five days, and Bosi said that would be long enough. Then the two men rowed ashore in a small boat and hid it in a secret cove. They walked for a while until they came to a house belonging to an old man and his wife, who had a good-looking daughter. The foster-brothers were given a friendly welcome and served with excellent wine in the evening.

Bosi gave the girl a cheerful smile, and she eyed him in return. A little

later they all went to sleep. Bosi went over to her bed, and she asked
what he wanted. He said he wanted her to put a ring on his stump. She
said she wondered what ring he could be talking about, and he asked
her didn't she have one? She answered that she hadn't any ring that
would fit him.

'I can widen it if it's too narrow,' he said.

'Where's that stump of yours? I've got a fair idea of what I can expect
from my narrow little ring.'

He told her to feel between his legs, but she pulled her hand back
and said his stump be damned.

'What does it remind you of?' he asked.

'My father's steel-yard with the ring broken off.'

'You're very witty,' said Bosi. He took a ring off his finger and gave
it her. She asked what he wanted in return.

'I want to put a stopper in your bung-hole,' he said.

'I can't think what you mean,' she said.

'Lie as open as you can,' he said.

She did as he asked, and he went between her legs and made a thrust
deep into her body, almost up under her ribs.

That made her jump, and she said, 'You've pushed the stopper right
through the hole, man.'

'I'll get it out again,' he said. 'How did you like that?'

'Nice as a drink of fresh mead,' she said. 'Keep the mop stirring in the
flue.'

He did his very best, and she got so warmed up that she began to feel
a bit sick, so she asked him to stop, and they took a rest. Then she
asked him who he was, and he told her. He asked her whether she was
by any chance on friendly terms with the king's daughter, Edda. She
answered that she often visited Edda's boudoir and was always given a
good welcome there.

'I'll take you into my confidence,' he said. 'I'm going to give you
three marks of silver, and in return you're to get the princess to join me
in the wood.'

Then he took three walnuts out of his purse, as bright as gold, and
gave them to her. She was to tell the princess that she knew a grove in
the forest where walnuts like these were plentiful.

The girl warned him that the princess wouldn't be afraid of just one man. 'There's a eunuch called Skalk who goes everywhere with her, and he's as strong as twelve men, and ready for anything.'

Bosi said he didn't mind as long as the odds were no worse than this.

Early next morning the girl went to see the princess, showed her the golden walnuts and told her she knew a place where they were plentiful.

'Let's go there right away and take Skalk with us,' said the princess, and that's what they did.

Bosi and Herraud were already in the grove and met them there. Bosi greeted the great lady and asked her why she was travelling with so small a retinue. She said there was no risk involved.

'That's what you think,' said Bosi. 'You've a choice of two things: either come with me willingly, or else I'll make you my wife right now, here in the wood.'

The eunuch asked who the dirty ruffian was that dared to babble on like that. Herraud told him to shut up and not behave like a fool. The eunuch hit out at Herraud with a heavy cudgel, but Herraud parried it with his shield. All the same, it was such a powerful blow that the shield was shattered. Herraud rushed at Skalk but he gave a good account of himself. There was a hard scuffle between them, but Skalk wouldn't budge an inch. Then Bosi came up to them and pulled Skalk's feet from under him, and after that they put a noose round his neck and hanged him on an oak tree.

Then Bosi took the princess and carried her in his arms down to the shore, where they rowed out to the ship and found Smid. The princess was heartbroken, but after Smid had had a word or two with her she soon cheered up.

And so they sailed back home to Gotaland.

14. A BATTLE

While all this was going on, Siggeir and Hrærek had gathered and fitted out a huge army. But King Godmund was not fit to travel because of the punch Herraud had given him, so the brothers were in sole charge. They set off from Glasir Plains with forty ships, but added a good many more as they went along. They went to Permia to

see their father, King Harek, just after Bosi and Herraud had left. By
now King Harek knew for certain that the foster-brothers had gone off
with his daughter. He had his own forces ready and fifteen large ships.
He joined his sons on their expedition, and between them they had
sixty ships in all, and with this fleet they sailed to Gotaland.

Now we come back to Herraud and Bosi, who had begun to gather
forces as soon as they arrived home, as they wanted to be ready in case
they were being followed. But they intended to celebrate the double
wedding as soon as they had the time and the opportunity. While they
were away Thvari had had a lot of spears, axes and arrows made, and
now the army began to grow.

Then they heard that King Harek and his sons were approaching the
coast, and things didn't look so good. Herraud ordered ships to be
launched to meet them. He had a large force of hand-picked men, but it
was much smaller than King Harek's. Smid attacked the king's ship,
while Bosi went for Hrærek, and Herraud for Siggeir. There's no need
to go into detail over what happened next. A fierce battle broke out,
with both sides eager to fight.

Soon after the battle had begun, Siggeir boarded Herraud's ship and
shortly afterwards killed one of his men. Herraud had a forecastleman
called Snidil, and he threw a spear at Siggeir, who caught it in flight and
hurled it back at him; the spear went right through Snidil and into the
prow, pinning him firmly to the timbers. Herraud turned to meet
Siggeir and lunged at him with a halberd. It went through his shield
but Siggeir gave it a powerful jerk so that Herraud lost hold of the
weapon. At the same time Siggeir hit back at Herraud, slicing off his
ear and a part of his helmet. Herraud grabbed a huge log that was lying
on the deck and hit him on the nose, knocking the vizor off the helmet
and breaking all his teeth, and his nose as well. Siggeir tumbled back-
wards into his own ship, and lay there unconscious for a long time.

Smid fought bravely, but King Harek managed to board his ship
with eleven men and they caused a great deal of damage. Then Smid
turned to meet him and lunged at him with a special short-sword that
Busla had given him, because Harek couldn't be hurt by ordinary
weapons. The blow caught him in the face, breaking all his teeth and
cutting his palate and lips. Blood poured out of his mouth. This blow

so upset King Harek that he turned into a flying dragon and spewed venom all over the ship, killing a number of men. Then he dived down at Smid and swallowed him in one gulp.

Next thing, they saw an enormous bird, called *skergipr*, flying down from the land. This bird had a huge horrible head and it's often compared with the devil himself. The bird attacked the dragon, and a savage struggle began. Eventually, they both came plunging down, the *skergipr* crashing into the sea and the dragon on to Siggeir's ship. Herraud was already there, cutting his way through with the log. He hit at Siggeir's ear, breaking his head into pieces and knocking him overboard, and he never came up again.

Then King Harek came to and turned himself into a boar. He snapped at Herraud with his teeth and tore the mailcoat off his body and bit into his breast, stripping off the nipple and all the flesh down to the bare bone. Herraud struck at the boar's snout, cutting clean through the head below the eyes. Herraud was now so exhausted that he fell over on his back. The boar trod on him but wasn't able to bite him because the snout had been cut off.

Next a monstrous bitch appeared on the deck. She had enormous teeth and tore a hole into the boar's groin. Then she unravelled his guts and jumped overboard. Harek reappeared in human form and dived into the sea after her. Both sank to the bottom of the sea and never came up again. It's thought very likely that this bitch would have been Busla, since she was never seen after that.

15. VICTORY

By this time Bosi had boarded Hrærek's ship and was fighting like a real hero. Then he saw his father floating on the water just beside the ship, so he dived in and helped him on board his own ship.

Hrærek had already boarded the ship and killed a good many men. Bosi was exhausted when he climbed aboard, but in spite of that he turned on Hrærek and hewed at his shield, splitting it in two and cutting off his leg at the ankle. The sword finished up in the yard-arm and broke in two. Hrærek hit back and struck at Bosi as he was turning round. The sword hit the helmet and ran down the shoulder, tearing the mailcoat and wounding him in the shoulder-blade, and so right down his back. All his clothes were torn off him, so he stood there stark-naked with the heel-bone sliced off his left foot. Bosi then seized a beam, but Hrærek tried to jump overboard, and was leaning against the bulwark when Bosi struck at him, severing the body, so that one part fell overboard, and the other into the ship. By this time most of their men had been killed, but those still alive were spared.

The foster-brothers now took a roll-call of their troops and there weren't more than a hundred men still able to fight. All the same, they had won a great victory, and now they shared out what they'd taken in the battle, and all the wounded men who could be were given treatment.

16. THE END OF THE STORY

After that Herraud and Bosi made arrangements for their weddings. There was plenty of all that was needed, and the feast lasted a month. When it was over, they gave all the guests splendid gifts as parting presents. Herraud became king of all the territories that his father had ruled over.

A little later they gathered their forces and went to Permia. Bosi demanded to be accepted as king there, because his wife Edda was the legal heir after her father. Bosi told the people that this would be the best way of compensating the country for the men he had killed. Then he could make them strong, with better laws and more justice. And since they had no leader now, the best solution they could find would be to make him their king. Edda was well-known to them and they knew all about her excellent qualities, so Bosi became the king of Permia.

Bosi had a son by the girl who had tempered his warrior for him. That son was called Svidi the Bold, and his son was Vilmund the Absentminded.

Bosi went east to Glasir Plains and made peace between King Godmund and Herraud.

Herraud and Hleid loved each other dearly, and their daughter was Thora Town-Hart, who married Ragnar Hairy-breeks.

According to legend, a small snake was found in the vulture's egg which Herraud and Bosi had fetched from Permia. It was golden in colour, and King Herraud give it to his daughter as a teething-gift. She put a piece of gold under the snake, and after that it grew and grew until it circled her bower. The snake was so savage that no one dared come near it except the king and the man who fed it. The snake ate an old ox for every meal, and everyone thought it an extremely evil creature. King Herraud made a solemn vow that he would only marry Thora to the man brave enough to go into the bower and destroy the snake, but no one had enough courage for this until Ragnar, son of Sigurd Hring, appeared on the scene. This Ragnar has since been known as Ragnar Hairy-breeks, and his nickname is taken from the clothes he had made for himself when he went to kill the snake.

And so we end the Saga of Stunt-Bosi.

Egil and Asmund

1. BRYNHILD

There was a king called Hertrygg who ruled over Russia, a large, well-populated country lying between Hunland and Novgorod. He was married and had two daughters, both called Hild. They were fine-looking, even-tempered girls, very well brought up, and the king was extremely fond of them.

Once when the king was away on a hunting trip, the elder Hild went with her maidens to a nut-grove. She was called Brynhild, and this was because she had been trained in the skills of knighthood. As the women were getting ready to go back home from the wood, a huge beast, called the *hjasi*, came up to them. This is an enormous, savage animal, and of all the beasts the *hjasi* has the longest life, which explains the saying that a very old man is 'as old as the *hjasi*'; it's shaped like a monstrous dog, but with ears so large they touch the ground. The women scattered in all directions as soon as they saw the creature, but the *hjasi* got hold of the princess and ran into the wood with her.

The maidens went back home and told what had happened. The king was terribly distressed by the news and had a search made for his daughter, but they could find no trace of her, anywhere. No one could tell him anything about her disappearance, and soon people began to lose interest in it.

So time passed till Christmas.

2. BEKKHILD

At Christmas the king held a magnificent feast. The younger Hild, a clever girl – they called her Bekkhild because of her skill at embroidery – used to sit in her boudoir. On the first day of Christmas the king sent for his daughter, who made herself ready and went into the street with her maidens escorted by some gentlemen of the court. As they were passing a certain garden they heard a great uproar and saw a terrible vulture flying overhead. Its wings seemed to extend over the entire city. Then a great darkness fell and the vulture grabbed the princess and flew away with her. It struck two of her servants dead, and all the others were shaken with terror.

The news soon reached the royal palace. The king was extremely distressed and said, 'There seems no end to our misfortunes. I can't see what can be behind these monsters. I want you all to know that anyone who cares to search for my daughter shall not only marry one if he finds them, but get a third of my kingdom as well. Even if the searcher finds them dead, he can still have the best earldom in the country and choose any woman he wants as his wife.'

Some people said that this was a generous offer but added that there was a great deal at stake. After Christmas everyone went back home, greatly disturbed by what had happened.

Winter passed, and the summer after. Late in the autumn it happened that a small ship, gold-painted above the water-line, put into the harbour. It had thirty men on board, not including servants. The king happened to be at the harbour, and these men went before him to present themselves. He responded in a friendly way to their greetings and asked who they were. Their leader replied that his name was Asmund and that he was known as the Berserks-Killer.

'How old are you?' said the king.

'Sixteen,' said Asmund.

'I've never seen a more useful looking fellow for your age,' said the king. 'Where have you come from?'

'A viking expedition,' said Asmund. 'But now winter's coming on and we'd like to have sanctuary here till spring. We're not short of money to pay our own way.'

The king said he was welcome to stay, so Asmund had his cargo unloaded, and they were given a fine house to store their goods. Asmund, however, spent most of the time drinking in the king's palace.

Asmund and his men got on well with everybody.

3. EGIL ONE-HAND

One day after Asmund had been staying there a month it happened that eighteen men came into the hall, every one of them wounded.

Their leader, Rognvald, was in charge of the king's defences. The king responded warmly to his greetings and asked who had given him such a rough handling.

'There's a man called Egil come to your country' said Rognvald 'a hard man to deal with. He's been plundering your kingdom, so I went against him with five well-equipped ships while he had just one ship and a crew of thirty. I didn't expect them to give me any trouble but the outcome of the battle was that I had to run for it, and all my men have been killed, apart from those here. He only has a single hand, and so he's known as Egil One-hand, but he manages to do more with the one that's missing than with the other. Just above the wrist there's a sword fixed, made by dwarfs, and there isn't a man alive can stand up to his strokes.'

With that Rognvald went to his seat and dropped down dead. 'The thought that your death won't be avenged is not to be borne,' said the king.

'The best way to repay your hospitality,' said Asmund, 'would be if I went to see this Egil.'

'I'd like that,' said the king. 'You can take as many men as you want.'

'I'm not in the habit of taking on extra men when the odds are fair,' said Asmund. 'But if Egil has more men than I have, the farmers are sure to help us.'

4. THE ENCOUNTER

Asmund set off to meet Egil, and told his men to row fully armed over to Egil's ship. Egil wasn't unprepared for this, and asked who was responsible for all that rowing.

Asmund gave his name. 'I've some business with you,' he added.

'Let's hear what you want,' said Egil.

'I want to exchange weapons with you,' said Asmund, 'and give you swords for axes.'

'We're not likely to refuse your offer,' said Egil. 'Do you have plenty of money on board?'

Asmund said he hadn't. 'We're hoping to put that right with your help. How do you plan to compensate the king for your plunderings?'

'We're not in the habit of paying out money for the odd sheep my lads take for the table,' said Egil.

'In that case we'll have to use force,' said Asmund. 'The king's sent me for your head.'

'He must be pretty anxious to get rid of you,' said Egil. 'Why shouldn't we become sworn-brothers? Then we can kill the king and marry his daughters.'

'They're not available at the moment, they've both been abducted,' said Asmund.

'It would be a pity if our men were to kill each other,' said Egil. 'Let's fight a duel instead.'

Asmund said he was ready enough for that. So they went ashore to try out each other's skill, and were just about evenly matched. In the evening they all sat down to a joint drinking feast, and after that they slept through the night.

Next morning Asmund and Egil took up their weapons again and set to, each destroying three of the other's shields.

When the sun was due south, Egil said, 'Do you want to go on with the game?'

'Nothing's been proved either way yet,' said Asmund, 'and the king isn't going to think my mission's been properly carried out if we stop now.'

'Just as you wish,' said Egil.

'How old are you?' asked Asmund.

'Eighteen,' said Egil.

'Pick up your weapons if you want to live longer,' said Asmund.

So they fought another round, and it seemed to them as if every stroke was a death-blow. When the sun was in the south-west, Egil said, 'I think it would be better for us to stop this game now.'

'You must be getting scared,' said Asmund, who had already received one wound.

'Look out for yourself then,' said Egil.

So they fought the third round. Asmund could do no more than defend his life, and he'd already been wounded three times. He realized that this wouldn't do, so he threw down his sword and flung himself at Egil. It was awkward for Egil to use the mutilated hand, and the scuffle took them all over the field. At last Egil fell, and by then each had torn off the other's helmet.

'My sword's not to hand,' said Asmund, 'and I can't be bothered to bite your throat.'

'You've not much choice in the matter,' said Egil.

'I'm going to take a chance,' said Asmund, and ran for his sword and then back to Egil who was lying as still as if he was having his hair cut.

Asmund said, 'You haven't any equal, Egil. Stand up now. I want to accept the offer you made, and become your sworn brother.'

'It worries me a lot,' said Egil, 'that I owe you my life.'

'I'm not going to kill you,' said Asmund, 'but I want you to come with me to the king.'

Then their men arrived on the scene and pleaded with them to be reconciled. So they shook hands and each swore to become the other's sworn brother according to ancient custom.

5. EAGLE-BEAK

They got ready for the voyage and went back to King Hertrygg. Asmund greeted the king, who received him kindly and asked if he had met Egil One-Hand.

Asmund said he certainly had. 'I've never met a braver man. He's offered to take Rognvald's place, and we'll defend your country together.'

'If you're both willing to swear an oath of loyalty and take his place, I'll accept this offer as a settlement,' said the king.

Asmund said he was willing to do that, and then Egil was called for and they were put in charge of the country's defences, and stayed there over winter.

At Christmas the king gave a feast, and on the first day he asked whether anyone there could tell him what had happened to his daughters, but no one could. Then the king repeated the offer he had made before.

Egil said, 'This is a chance for a brave man to earn some money.'

After Christmas all the guests went back home.

Soon after mid-winter Egil and Asmund launched their ship and selected a crew of twenty-four. They put a man called Viglogi in charge of those who were left behind. Egil and Asmund announced that they were not coming back till they had found the king's daughters, dead or alive. Then they put out to sea, though they had no idea of where they should go. They spent the summer exploring outlying islands, skerries and mountains, and in the autumn they had reached as far north as Jotunheim. There they sailed close in by a forest, hauled their ship ashore and made themselves comfortable.

The foster-brothers told their men to stay there over the winter. 'Egil and I are going to explore this country,' said Asmund, 'and if we don't come back next summer, you're free to go wherever you like.'

They set off into the wood, shooting deer and birds for food. But months passed by, and sometimes they had no food at all. One day they came to a valley with a river flowing through it and low grassy banks on either side. The hill-sides were wooded below and rocky higher up. There they saw a great number of she-goats and some well-fed males. They rounded up the herd and got hold of one of the fat goats with the idea of slaughtering it. Then they heard shouting up the slope, and all the goats scattered and they lost hold of the one they'd caught. They saw a monster up among the rocks, broader than it was high. It spoke in a shrill, bell-like voice and asked who was so bold that he dared steal one of the Queen's goats.

'Who are you, O beautiful, bed-worthy lady? Where's your Queen's country?'

'My name's Skin-Beak,' she said, 'I'm the daughter of Queen Eagle-Beak who rules over Jotunheim. Her residence isn't very far from here, and you'd better go and see her before you start stealing things.'

'You're absolutely right,' said Asmund, and gave her a gold ring.

'I daren't accept this,' she said, 'I'm sure my mother will say that's my bed-money.'

'I'm not in the habit of taking back my gifts,' said Asmund, 'but we'd like you to find us a place to stay.'

She went ahead of them home to her mother, who asked her why she was so late. Skin-Beak said she had found two men who needed hospitality. 'One of them gave me a gold ring and asked me to find them lodgings,' she said.

'Why did you take money from them?'

'I was hoping you might repay them for it,' said Skin-Beak.

'Why didn't you invite them here?'

'I wasn't sure how you'd take it,' she said.

'Ask them over,' said Eagle-Beak.

Skin-Beak ran back to them and said, 'My mother wants you to come and see her. You'd better be ready with the news, because she's very sharp about most things.'

So they went to see the old hag. She asked them their names, and they told her. She could hardly take her eyes off Egil. They said they'd not eaten for a whole week. The hag was skimming the milk. She had fifty goats yielding as much as cows, and an enormous cauldron, big enough to hold all this milk. She had a vast wheat-field too, and every day she took from it so much meal that the gruel she made with it filled the cauldron, and this was the food she and her daughter lived on.

'Skin-Beak,' she said, 'you'd better get some brushwood and make a good fire. Our hospitality wouldn't be up to much if we only offered them gruel to eat.'

Skin-Beak wasted no time, but even so her mother told her to hurry up and serve the food that was already cooked. So some game and venison appeared on the table.

The hag said, 'Let's not sit around saying nothing, even though the hospitality does leave something to be desired. It'll be a long while before the gruel's ready. Now, Asmund, you can tell us the story of your life, and then Egil can tell us his. After that I'll entertain you at table with some stories about my own adventures. I'm curious to hear about your family background and the reason for your travels.'

6. ARAN

Asmund began his story: There was a king called Ottar who ruled over Halogaland. He was married to Sigrid, daughter of Earl Ottar of Jutland in Denmark, and they had a son called Asmund. He was a fine big fellow, and while he was still young he was trained in all kinds of skills. When he was twelve he was considered a better man than anyone else in the land.

G

Asmund had a good many playmates. One day when they'd gone riding into the forest, Asmund saw a hare and set his hounds on it. The hare ran away and the hounds couldn't catch up with it, but Asmund didn't give up, and when his horse collapsed from exhaustion Asmund ran with the hounds after the hare. In the end the hare jumped off a sea-cliff. Asmund turned back to look for his horse but he couldn't find it. Dusk had already fallen, so Asmund had to spend the night there, but in the morning a heavy mist had risen so he had no idea where he was.

For three days Asmund was utterly lost in the wood, but then he saw a man coming towards him. This was a tall, handsome man, with a fine head of yellow silken hair, and he was wearing a scarlet cloak. It seemed to Asmund that he'd never seen a finer looking man. They greeted each other, and Asmund asked the stranger's name. He said he was called Aran, the son of King Rodian of Tartary. 'I've been on a viking expedition,' he added.

'How old are you?' asked Asmund.

'Twelve,' said Aran.

'There can't be many like you,' said Asmund.

'Back home I had no equal,' said Aran, 'and that's why I made a solemn vow not to go back until I'd found someone as good as myself, and the same age. Now, I've heard about a man called Asmund, the son of the King of Halogaland. Can you by any chance tell me anything about him? I've been told that there shouldn't be much between us.'

'I know him pretty well,' said Asmund. 'He's talking to you now.'

'That's a bit of luck,' said Aran. 'And now we'd better try each other out.'

Asmund said he was ready enough for that, so they performed every athletic feat which was known to young men in those days. They were so equally matched there was no choosing between them. Next they wrestled, and there was a hard tussle between them, but it was impossible to tell which was the stronger. When they separated, they were both exhausted.

Then Aran said to Asmund, 'We must never test each other's skill with weapons, because that would only lead to both our deaths. I'd like us to enter a sworn-brotherhood, each of us pledging himself to avenge the other, and sharing equally each other's money, now and in the future.'

It was also a part of their pact that the one who lived the longer should raise a burial mound over the one who was dead, and place in it as much money as he thought fit; and the survivor was to sit in the mound over the dead for three nights, but after that he would be free to go away.

Then they each opened a vein and mixed their blood, which was regarded as an oath. Aran invited Asmund to go with him down to the ships to see what a splendid outfit he had. Since Asmund was staying at that time in Jutland with his grandfather, Earl Ottar, he did as Aran wanted.

7. ARAN'S DEATH

They went down to Aran's ships; ten longships he had, all manned with good fighting men. Aran gave Asmund a half-share in all his ships and forces. Asmund wanted them to sail first to Halogaland to get his own ships and men, but Aran insisted on sailing first to his own country and going from there to Halogaland for the people to see that they were no mere beggars. Asmund said he could have it his own way and so they put to sea with a fair wind.

Asmund asked whether King Rodian had any other children. Aran said he had another son who was called Herraud. 'His mother's the daughter of the King of Hunland. Herraud's a brave man, very popular, and heir to the throne of Hunland. My father has two brothers, Hrærek and Siggeir, both berserks, very difficult to deal with, and pretty unpopular among the people. The king puts a lot of trust in them, because they do everything he tells them. They often go plundering and bring back treasures for the king.'

There's nothing more to tell of their voyage until they reached King Rodian's harbour, where they saw twelve warships and two dragon-headed longships, so splendid they'd never seen anything like them before. These ships belonged to two brothers from Ethiopia, called

Bull-Bear and Visin, sons of Earl Gorm. They'd killed King Rodian, laid much of the country waste and created utter havoc.

When the sworn-brothers heard of this, they had the alarm sounded, and as soon as the people realized that Aran had arrived they flocked to him in large numbers. The marauders rushed down to their ships and a ferocious and deadly battle broke out. For a long time the issue hung in the balance. Aran jumped on board Bull-Bear's ship and laid all about him so that everyone on board began to fall back. Bull-Bear turned to meet him, so Aran struck a blow at his bald pate, but the sword failed to bite into it and dust scattered from the skull and the sword broke at the hilt. Bull-Bear hit back at Aran's shield, splitting it right through and wounding him badly in the chest. A broken anchor was lying on the deck. Aran picked it up and drove it deep into Bull-Bear's head and then pushed him overboard, and Bull-Bear sank down to the sea-bottom.

Visin boarded Asmund's ship and hurled two spears simultaneously at him. Asmund tried to parry one with his shield, but it ran right through the shield and into Asmund's elbow, sticking firm into the bone. But Asmund caught the other spear in flight and hurled it back at Visin straight into his mouth, sinking it up to the middle of the shaft. The spear ran into the mast as far as the barb, with Visin dangling from it, dead. After that the vikings surrendered, and Asmund had them all killed and thrown overboard. Aran and Asmund went into the town, and the people were very content to see Aran; their wounds were seen to, and afterwards Aran was given the title of king. Then he announced his agreement with Asmund, and gave him a half-share in everything he owned.

Less than a month after their arrival Aran died suddenly one day as he was going into his palace. The corpse was dressed for burial according to custom. Asmund had a burial mound raised over Aran and beside the corpse he put in the mound Aran's horse with a saddle and bridle, his banners and armour, his hawk and hound. Aran was sitting on a chair in full armour.

Asmund had another chair brought into the mound and sat himself down there, and after the mound was covered up. During the first night Aran got up from his chair and killed the hawk and the hound and ate them. On the second night he got up again from his chair, and killed the horse and tore it into pieces; then he took great bites at the horseflesh with his teeth, the blood streaming down from his mouth all the while he was eating. He offered to let Asmund share his meal, but Asmund said nothing. The third night Asmund became very drowsy, and the first thing he knew, Aran had got him by the ears and torn them off. So Asmund drew his short sword and sliced off Aran's head, then he got some fire and burnt Aran to ashes. Asmund went to the rope and was hauled out of the mound, which was then covered up again.

Asmund took all the treasures from the mound with him.

8. THE BERSERKS

A little later Asmund called the people to a meeting and asked them whether they intended to honour the agreement he had made with Aran. Not many of them were in favour of the proposal; only the men Aran had given to Asmund were ready to support him.

At this point they happened to look out to sea and saw some ships sailing in. The leaders of this fleet were berserks, the brothers Hrærek and Siggeir. The people ashore weren't too happy about this. Asmund offered to be their leader, but no one was willing to put up a fight, so Asmund went back to his ships with his men.

When the berserks knew what had happened they claimed the whole country as their own. Asmund told them about his agreement with Aran and said half the country belonged to him. The berserks told him to go away if he wanted to stay alive. Asmund challenged either of them to a duel, with the kingdom as the stake, but they shouted him down and told their men to get ready for a fight. A fierce battle began. Asmund had a smaller force, and the people didn't dare to give him any help, so all his men were killed, and he himself was taken captive. This happened just towards evening.

The berserks decided that Asmund should be executed the following morning on top of Aran's mound and given to Odin as a victory offering. So Asmund was tied to the windlass, but all the men went ashore to see to their wounds and slept in the camp overnight. The brothers were sleeping in a small tent some distance away from the main camp and had only a few men with them.

Now we go back to Asmund, still tied to the windlass. He noticed an iron-lock jutting out from it. This had been given a great blow which had left a rough sharp edge on the iron. Asmund rubbed the rope against this and managed to cut it through as the edge was so sharp. Now that his hands were free he broke the shackles off his feet.

The wind was blowing from the sea, so Asmund cut the anchor line and the ship drifted right up under the forest. In no time he was ashore, and it occurred to him that he might play a bit of a joke on the berserks before making off into the forest. So he made his way to their tent and pulled it down on top of them. Those inside jumped to their feet, but couldn't get out as the tent got in their way. Asmund struck Hrærek in the head splitting it down to the jaw. Siggeir managed to get out and tried to run into the forest, but Asmund chased after him, and when Siggeir stumbled Asmand struck at his back just below its narrowest part, slicing it clean through. After that Asmund went into the wood, having already killed ten men as well as the berserks. A search was made for him but he couldn't be found.

Before the day was over Herraud arrived with twenty ships, and everybody was very relieved to see him. He had already heard what had happened, and now he called the people to a meeting where he announced his ownership of the kingdom and asked to be accepted as king. No one spoke up against him, so he was made king over the whole country. Those who had supported the berserks were driven away, and Herraud took their property.

Then Asmund went to see King Herraud and greeted him, and the king asked who he was. Asmund told him, and Herraud asked whether he was the man who had killed the berserks. Asmund said he was.

'Why have you come to me then?' asked the king.

'I couldn't think of anything better,' said Asmund, 'and it seemed to me that I'd dropped a good thing into your lap. I came to see you since I knew very well I couldn't escape from you. Now I want to know what's going to happen to me. I'll defend myself while I can and try to save my life, but I'd accept a better choice if it were offered.'

'I've been told about your agreement with Aran,' said Herraud, 'and it seems a good idea to take you in my brother's place. In my opinion we're well rid of the berserks you killed.'

So Asmund stayed with Herraud, and they got on well together. Asmund asked Herraud to provide him with some ships as he wanted to go plundering. Herraud told him to choose his own ships and as many men as he liked. He also invited Asmund to come and stay with him whenever he wanted. Asmund picked thirty of Herraud's men and chose a ship. He and Herraud parted the best of friends, each vowing to treat the other as his own brother wherever they might meet again.

From then on Asmund was known as the Berserks-Killer. This is the end of my story, because I am the same man as Asmund.'

'I think that was a very striking story,' said the old hag. 'How's the gruel getting on, my girl?'

'It's on the boil,' said Skin-Beak.

'It'll be a long while before it's ready,' said the queen. 'And what can you tell us, Egil?'

'Here's the beginning of my story,' said Egil.

9. THE GIANT

There was a king called Hring who ruled over the Smalands. He was married to Ingibjorg, the daughter of Earl Bjarkmar of Gotaland. They had two children, a son called Egil, and a daughter called Æsa. Egil grew up at his father's court until he was twelve years old. He was quite a handful, troublesome, ambitious, and very difficult to deal with. He used to go around with a crowd of boys and often went with them into the woods to shoot deer and birds.

There was a large lake in the wood, with a number of islands in it, and Egil and his companions used to go swimming there as they'd become very clever at all kinds of sports. One day Egil asked the other boys which of them could swim the farthest out into the lake. The outermost island was so far away from land that to see it they had to climb the highest trees. So they set out swimming across the lake, thirty of them in all. Everybody agreed that no one should risk going out farther than he felt safe. They went on swimming out into the lake, and some of the sounds between the islands were very wide. Egil was the fastest swimmer and no one could keep up with him. When they had swum a long way from the shore, a mist came down on them so dark that none of them could see the others. Then a cold wind sprang up, and they all lost their bearings. Egil had no idea what had happened to his companions, and wandered about in the water for two days. At last he came to land but now he was so weak that he had to crawl ashore. He covered himself with moss and lay there overnight and in the morning he was feeling a bit warmer.

Then a great giant came out of the wood, and picked Egil up and tucked him under his arm. 'It's a good thing we've met, Egil,' he said. 'Now I'm offering you one of two choices: either I kill you right away, or else you're to swear an oath to look after my goats for as long as I live.'

Egil didn't waste much time deciding, finding himself in this predicament.

They travelled for a good many days, and in the end they came to the cave where the giant had his residence. The giant owned a hundred billy-goats, besides a good many she-goats and it was a matter of life and death to him that their number was kept up. Egil started herding the goats and they gave him plenty of trouble. So it went on for quite a time, but after Egil had been there for a year he ran away. As soon as the giant discovered this, after Egil he went, being so clever that he could trace footprints as readily in water as in snow. After Egil had been gone four days the giant found him in a cave.

The giant said that Egil had treated him worse than he'd deserved. 'So now you're going to get something that'll be all the worse for you,' he added.

He took two stones, each of them weighing forty pounds, fastened them with iron clamps to Egil's feet, and then told him he could drag this load behind him; and that's what Egil had to put up with for seven years.

The giant was always on his guard, so Egil couldn't see any chance of killing him.

10. ESCAPE

One day when Egil had gone to look for his goats he came across a cat in the wood. He managed to catch it and brought it home with him. It was late in the evening when he came back home, and the fire was smouldering into ashes. The giant asked him why he was so late getting back, and Egil answered that he wasn't all that lightly dressed for walking, and anyway the goats were running all over the place.

'It's a marvel to me,' said the giant, 'how you can find what you're looking for in the dark!'

'That's because of my gold eyes,' said Egil.

'Have you got any other eyes, apart from the ones I've seen?' asked the giant.

'I certainly have,' said Egil.

'Let's have a look at these treasures, then,' said the giant.

'You won't steal them from me?' said Egil.

'They wouldn't be any use to me,' said the giant.

'They're no use to anyone,' said Egil, 'unless I fit them on.'

Then Egil lifted the hem of his cloak and the giant saw into the cat's eyes across the fire and they glittered like two stars.

'That's a treasure worth having,' said the giant. 'Would you sell me these eyes?'

'I'd be all the poorer for it,' said Egil. 'But if you'd set me free and take off these shackles, then I'd sell them to you.'

'Could you fit them well enough,' asked the giant, 'for me to get the full benefit of them?'

'I'll do my best,' said Egil. 'But you'll find the operation a bit painful, as I'll have to lift your eyelids quite a lot to fix the eyes where they ought to be. You'll always have to take them out as soon as it grows light, and only put them in after dark. Now I've got to tie you to this column.'

'You want to kill me,' said the giant, 'that's a mean trick to play!'

'I'd never do such a thing!' said Egil.

So they made a bargain, and the giant took the shackles off him.

'You've done the right thing,' said Egil, 'and now I'll make you a promise – I'll serve you for the rest of your life.'

Then Egil tied the giant to the column and took a forked rod and drove it into the eyes so that they lay bare on the giant's cheeks. The giant jerked so violently with the pain that he snapped the ropes he had been tied with. He fumbled about after Egil and tore the cloak right off him.

'Your luck's run out,' said Egil. 'The gold eyes have fallen into the fire and now they'll be no use to either of us.

'You've played a dirty trick on me,' said the giant. 'But you'll starve to death in here, and never get out.'

The giant made a rush for the door and locked it securely, and Egil didn't feel too hopeful about his future. He had to stay in the cave four nights without any food and with the giant guarding it all the time.

Then Egil made up his mind what to do. He slaughtered the biggest goat and flayed the skin off, then crept into the skin and sewed it up as tightly as he could.

On the morning of the fourth day Egil drove the goats to the entrance. The giant had placed his thumb against the lintel and his little finger on the doorstep, and the goats had to pass between. Their footsteps echoed on the cave floor.

The giant said, 'It's a sign of windy weather when the hooves of my goats start knocking.'

The goats ran out between his fingers, with Egil bringing up the rear. There wasn't a sound from his hooves.

'You're moving very slowly today, Horny-Beard,' said the giant, 'and you're pretty thick about the shoulders.'

Then he took hold of the goat's wool with both hands, and gave Egil such a shock that he tore the skin and so got away free.

'It was lucky for you that I'm blind,' said the giant. 'All the same it's a pity we have to part without your getting any present from me in recognition of your long service. So have this gold ring from me.'

It was extremely valuable, and Egil thought it a very fine ring, so he stretched out his hand for it. When the giant felt him take the ring, he pulled Egil towards him and struck at him, cutting off his right ear. It was lucky for Egil the giant was blind. Egil cut the giant's right hand off and got the ring.

'I'm going to keep my word,' said Egil, 'and I won't kill you. You'll just have to put up with the agony, and may your last day be your worst.'

With that they parted, and Egil went on his way. For some time he slept out of doors in the wood. When he came out of the wood he saw some viking ships. Their leader was a man called Borgar. Egil joined them and proved himself the bravest of men. They spent the summer plundering, and at Svia Skerries they fought a berserk called Glammad. He had one excellent weapon, a halberd, which could pick out any opponent as soon as the bearer knew his name. Soon after the battle started Glammad jumped aboard Borgar's ship and ran him through with the halberd. Egil was standing nearby with his spear broken off the shaft. He raised the shaft and drove it hard against Glammad's ear, forcing him overboard. Glammad sank to the bottom with his halberd, and neither of them ever came up again. Then the vikings stopped fighting and made Egil their leader. He picked out thirty-two men, and went plundering in the Baltic. A good many things happened on his campaign.

11. THE DWARF

On one occasion Egil lay at anchor in a certain harbour because of bad sailing weather. He went ashore by himself and came to a clearing in a wood. He saw a mound in the clearing and on it a huge giant fighting a giantess over a gold ring. She was much weaker than her opponent, who was giving her a rough time. She was wearing a very short dress, and her genitalia were very conspicuous. She tried to hang on to the ring as best she could. Egil struck at the giant, aiming for the shoulder, but the giant turned quickly so the sword slid down the arm, slicing off the biceps: this piece was so big, one man couldn't have lifted it. The giant struck back at Egil and caught him on the arm, cutting it off at the wrist, so that the sword and the hand fell to the ground together. The giant got ready to strike at Egil a second time so Egil had no choice but to run. The giant went after him into the wood, but Egil managed to escape and so they parted. Egil went back to his men with one hand missing and they sailed away.

Egil suffered a lot of pain from the arm. Two days later they came to another harbour and spent a night there. Egil couldn't stand the pain any longer so he got out of bed and took a walk into the forest. He came to a stream and seemed to get some relief from keeping the arm in the water and letting it wash over the wound. Then Egil saw a dwarf child coming out of a rock with a pail to fetch water. Egil picked a gold ring off his finger with his teeth and let it slip into the bucket, and the child ran with it back into the rock.

A little later a dwarf came out of the rock and asked who'd been so kind to his child. Egil told him his name and added that the way things stood, gold wasn't much use to him.

'I'm sorry to hear that,' said the dwarf. 'Come with me into the rock.'

So that's what Egil did, and the dwarf started dressing the stump. Soon the pain had completely gone, and in the morning the wound was healed. Then the dwarf set about making him a sword, and from the hilt he made a socket so deep, it reached up to the elbow, where it could be clasped to the arm. So now Egil found it as easy to strike with the sword as if he still had the whole arm. The dwarf also gave him a good many other valuable things, and they parted the best of friends. Then Egil went back to his men.

'So this,' said Egil, 'is my story up to date, because I'm the same man as this Egil whose story I've been telling.'

'You seem to have got yourself into plenty of trouble,' said the queen. 'How is the gruel getting on, my girl?'

'I think it's properly cooked now,' she replied, 'but it's far too hot for anyone to eat while it's like this.'

'I think you can take it,' said the queen, 'that it'll have cooled by the time I've told my tale, though nothing very much has ever happened to me.'

12. QUEEN EAGLE-BEAK'S TALE

There was a giant called Oskrud, who came from Jotunheim. His wife was called Kula, and he had two brothers called Gaut and Hildir. My father Oskrud had eighteen daughters by his wife, and I was the youngest. Everybody agreed I was the best-looking of them all. My

father and mother took ill and died, and then they were put under-
ground and given back to the trolls. We sisters inherited all the money
they left, but Gaut and Hildir took the kingdom. They got on badly
together.

My father had owned three remarkable treasures: a horn, a chess set,
and a gold ring. The brothers grabbed the horn and the chess set, but
we sisters managed to hold on to the ring, which was a very valuable
thing to have. My sisters used to bully me and I had to wait on them all.
Whenever I tried to argue they used to hit me. In the end I felt I couldn't
bear it any longer so I made a vow to Thor to give him any goat he'd
choose to have if he'd even things up between my sisters and me.

Thor paid us a visit, and went to bed with my eldest sister and lay
with her all night, but my other sisters were so jealous of her that they
killed her in the morning. Thor did the same thing to all my sisters, he
slept with them all in turn, and they were all killed. But each of them
managed to utter a curse on the next, that if she had a child by Thor it
would neither grow nor thrive.

Eventually Thor slept with me and gave me this daughter you can
see, and the curse has worked well enough on her because she's a yard
shorter now than when she was born. Thor gave me everything the
sisters left, and he's always been very helpful to me. So I got all the
money, but ever since I've been driven by a sexual urge so strong that I
don't seem able to live without a man.

One of the men I had to have was Hring, son of the king of the
Smalands. So I set out to see him, but he'd gone off to Gotaland to ask
for the hand of Ingibjorg, the daughter of Earl Bjarkmar. I hurried on
my way but when I arrived in Gotaland, Hring was already celebrating
his wedding-feast and his bride was about to be led into the hall. I lay
down in the street intending to play her some dirty trick, but she
noticed me first and gave me a kick that broke both my thigh-bones.
Then she was led into the hall to her seat. I followed her inside and
turned myself into a fly, and crept under her clothes with the idea of
ripping her belly open at the groin. But she recognized me right away
and struck at my flank with a knife handle and broke three of my ribs,
so I thought I'd better get out of there.

The day passed, and when the bride was being led to her bed and the bridegroom ushered out of the hall, I picked him up in my arms, and it seemed to me as if I was running down to the sea-cliffs to drown him so no one else would be able to enjoy him. But while I thought I was throwing him off the cliffs, all I did was fling him behind the bed-curtain. He landed on the bed alongside his bride, and I was captured, with no hope of escape. To save my life I was to go to the Underworld and fetch three treasures: a cloak that fire couldn't burn, a drinking horn that could never be emptied, and a chess set that would play by itself whenever anyone challenged it.

13. THE UNDERWORLD

So I went down to the Underworld and saw King Snow, and for sixty goats and a pound of gold I bought the horn from him. But a poison-cup the size of twelve casks had been prepared for his queen, and I had to drink this on her behalf as well. Ever since then I've always been a bit troubled with heartburn.

From there I went to Mount Lucanus where I found three women (if you could call them women, for I looked like a baby compared with them), in charge of the chess set. I managed to get half of the chess set off them, but when they found it missing and realized it was me, they asked me to give it back. I refused and challenged any one of them to take it away from me, staking the chess set against all the gold I could carry. They thought this wouldn't be too hard for them, and so one of them made for me, grabbed hold of my hair and tore half of it off and the left ear and the whole cheek with it. She was hard on me, but I didn't give in, I put my fingers into her eyes and gouged them both out. Then I tried to throw her, but she caught her foot in a rock crevice so I dislocated her hip joint. With that we parted.

Then the second sister rushed at me and gave me a punch on the nose, so that she broke it. It's been regarded as rather a blemish on my looks ever since, and I lost three teeth as well. I got hold of her breasts and tore them both off down to the ribs and then the flesh of her belly and the entrails too.

Next the third sister attacked me, the smallest of them. I meant to gouge her eyes out just as I'd done to the other, but she bit off two of my fingers. I put her down with a heel-throw, and she fell flat on her back. She begged for mercy, and I told her that I'd only spare her life if she gave me the whole chess set. She didn't waste any time over that. Then I told her to get up, and as a parting gift she gave me a magic glass. If a man looks into it, I can give him the shape of anyone I choose. If I want I can blind the man who looks into it.

Next I went to the Underworld to fetch the cloak, and there I met the Chief of Darkness. As soon as he saw me he said he wanted to sleep with me. I guessed he must be Odin because he only had one eye. He told me I could have the cloak if I was willing to fetch it from where it was kept. I had to jump across a huge fire to get it. First I slept with Odin, then I jumped over the fire and got the cloak, but ever since I've had no skin to my body.

After doing all this I went back home to Hring and Ingibjorg and gave them the treasures. But before we parted I had to swear an oath never to avenge myself on them. So, not feeling very happy about the affair, I came back to my own home. For the rest of my life I'll remember that girl in Gotaland. Later I'll tell you about the little games I've had to play with my brothers. How's the gruel getting on, my girl?

'I think it's just about cool enough,' she said.

'Serve it up then,' said the hag.

After they had finished their meal the foster-brothers were shown to their bed, and they slept through the night.

14. RECOVERY

In the morning the brothers woke up early. The old hag joined them, and when they asked her what time it was, she told them that they could stay there all day. So they got up and dressed. The old hag was very hospitable. They sat down to a meal, and now she offered them fine ale and good cooking, and inquired where they were going and what business they had. They told her all about their business and asked her whether she could give them any idea of what had happened to King Hertrygg's daughters.

'I don't know how successful you'll be in your search for them,' she said. 'But first of all, I'd better tell you what happened after the death of the giant Oskrud. The brothers didn't agree about which of them should be king, they both felt they had the right. Anyway, they agreed that the one who could get the more nobly born and talented princess should be the king. Gaut was the first to go and carried off King Her-trygg's elder daughter Hild; then Hildir went and carried off Bekkhild. Both girls are here now in Jotunheim, but I don't think they'll be easy to get at. They're to be married at Christmas, and all the giants will be gathered to decide which of the sisters has the greater skill.

'Things are looking up,' said Asmund, 'now we know where the sisters are. It would make all the difference if you'd help us.'

'The only reason why I keep up my family ties with Gaut and Hildir,' she said, 'is so that I shouldn't be under any obligation to them. It's due more to my own integrity than to anything on their part. You'd better take a rest here for today, and I'll show you my treasures.'

They found this very agreeable. When the table had been cleared, the old hag led them into a large side-chamber off the main cave. Inside there were a number of boxes which she unlocked, full of a great many rare and precious things. They got a great deal of pleasure from looking at them. Finally, the old hag picked up a small casket and opened it. A sweet fragrance came from it, and inside, Egil recognized his hand with his gold ring on the finger. It seemed to him as if the hand was still warm and steaming, and the veins were throbbing.

'Do you happen to know anything about this hand, Egil?' asked the old hag.

'I certainly do,' said Egil, 'and I know this gold ring my mother once gave me. But how did you come by my hand?'

'I can tell you about that,' said the old hag. 'My brother Gaut came and asked me to sell him my precious gold ring, but I wouldn't part with it. Some time later when my daughter was out tending the goats, he went to her and gave her a certain drink. This started her screaming and she couldn't be stopped until I brought the ring to her where she was lying on top of a mound. But when I arrived with the ring Gaut turned up and wanted to take it away from me. I stood up to him, and there was quite a struggle between us. I was just about to loose my hold on the ring when a stranger came out of the wood, and he seemed

very much like you, Egil. He took a great swing at the giant but the
giant cut off his hand, and after that both of them ran off into the wood.
I picked up the hand and ever since then I've looked after it and kept it
wrapped in life-herbs so that it wouldn't die. I think we both agree,
Egil, that this man must have been you. If you'll risk letting me re-open
the wound, I'll try to graft the hand on to the arm.'

'I don't see any risk in that,' said Egil. She took the socket off his
arm and deadened the arm so that Egil didn't feel any pain when she
trimmed the stump. Then she put life-herbs on it, wrapped it in silk
and held it firmly for the rest of the day. Egil could feel how the life
flowed in. The old hag put him to bed and told him to stay there until
his hand was healed. It was fully healed in three days, and now he
found the hand no stiffer than it had been when the arm was still whole,
though it seemed to have a red thread around it.

They asked the old hag what she would advise them to do, and she
told them to stay there till the wedding.

'My partner, Skrogg, lives not far from here and if we manage to
outwit my brothers, I'd like Skrogg and myself to profit from it.' So
time passed till Christmas.

15. THE WEDDING

Now we take up the story at the point where the brothers Gaut and
Hildir called the giants together to a meeting, to which they came from
all over Jotunheim. Skrogg, as the giants' lawman, was there as well. The
two princesses were led before the gathering with the master-pieces
they had created. Brynhild had made a carpet with this remarkable
property, that you could fly on it through the air and land wherever
you wanted. You could even carry a heavy load on it. Bekkhild had
made a shirt and there wasn't a weapon that could bite it, nor would
anyone wearing it ever get tired swimming.

Now an argument started about which of the sisters had shown the
greater skill. The final decision was a matter for all the giants, but they
couldn't reach an agreement, so Skrogg was asked to make the award.
His verdict was that Brynhild was the more beautiful of the two, and
that her carpet was made with the greater skill, 'and so Gaut shall be the

H

king and marry Brynhild, and each of the brothers rule over half the kingdom.'

After that the assembly broke up.

The brothers invited the leaders and all the most important people to the double wedding.

Skrogg came back home and told the old hag what had happened at the assembly and also when the wedding was to be. They talked things over for a long time and she told him that she wanted to help the brothers. She asked him to come with a large following and anything else they needed. Skrogg said he would do as she wanted.

When the time had come for the wedding the old hag, and the foster-brothers with her, got ready to go. One of them was to be called Fjalar and the other Frosti. She made them look into the mirror, and then they seemed as huge as giants, although much better-looking. She provided them with the right sort of clothes, and so they travelled on till they came to the brothers' residence called Gjallandi Bridge. The giants were drinking; and when the old hag walked into the cave, each glanced at the other. She went up to Gaut and gave him a respectful greeting.

He made a proper acknowledgement, 'This is something that's never happened before, your paying us a visit,' he said.

'Things aren't quite as they should be,' she answered. 'Relations have been pretty cool between us till now, and I won't deny that I'm to blame for that. I realize now, my dear Gaut, that you've good luck on your side: you've found an excellent wife, and as my contribution I'd like to offer something we've been quarrelling over in the past. I'm going to give you that fine ring, as an ideal bed-gift for your wife, and my friendship with it. We owe it to our family ties to be generous to each other.'

Gaut said he was truly grateful. '. . . and, by the way, where did you find these good-looking men?'

She told him they were the sons of King Dumb of the Dumb Sea, 'and you won't easily find anyone in Jotunheim to equal them, particularly in matters of etiquette. I'd meant them to be in attendance at your wedding.

Then she handed the ring over to Gaut who thanked her for it. She was to serve at the wedding, everything was to be done exactly as Fjalar and Frosti wanted it and they were given keys to all the money boxes.

The guests were now beginning to arrive and soon there was a huge gathering. The old hag was in charge, and everything had to be done according to her instructions. Skrogg the Lawman was the most respected of all the honoured guests.

The old hag explained in a whisper to the sisters who her companions were. 'So you can cheer up, now,' she added.

This made them very happy for they hadn't felt particularly enthusiastic about their wedding. But the giants were delighted to see them in a cheerful mood and thanked their kinswoman for her good services. When all the guests had been settled and the brothers had sat down, the brides were led inside. The giants were making boorish jokes in loud voices. Skrogg the Lawman was sitting on one side with the farmers, and Gaut and Hildir on the opposite bench with their own followers. Eagle-Beak was sitting next to the brides, and helped by some other huge ladies she gave them advice about how they should conduct themselves. Fjalar and Frosti served the ladies and there was no shortage of strong drink.

So the evening wore on and the guests were becoming quite drunk. Then Eagle-Beak got to her feet and called the lawman and the foster-brothers over to her, telling them to bring in the wedding presents. So the magic carpet, the shirt, the fine chess set that belonged to the brothers, the excellent ring that had belonged to Eagle-Beak, and many other things of value were carried into the cave. Skrogg the Lawman handed over the wedding presents, and the old hag took them into her charge. She spread the carpet on the ground, put the other treasures on top of it, and told her daughter Skin-Beak to fetch the gold and silver.

Eagle-Beak went back into the cave and asked Frosti to come with her. They went to the place where Gaut and Brynhild were supposed to sleep. She told Frosti that behind the bed-post he'd find Gaut's famous sword, the only weapon that could wound him. She also said that Fjalar and Hildir would be meeting again in another place, and warned the foster-brothers to get ready for a test of their manhood.

After that Eagle-Beak went back to the main cave and called out that it was bed-time for the brides. Fjalar and Frosti took the brides by the hand and settled them down on the carpet. Then the old hag made the carpet take off. She gave her daughter the mirror and told her to go to the entrance of the cave and hold the mirror to the face of all those who came out. The sisters soared in the air on the carpet, along with everything that was on it.

Now a lively dance started up in the cave as the bridegrooms were about to be led outside.

16. CASUALTIES

The cave had three doors. Skrogg the Lawman with his party was in charge of one of them and Skin-Beak was in charge of the door through which the common people went. The bridegrooms were led through the third door and just outside it were two smaller caves on either side, hung with fine tapestries, where they were to sleep.

When the two giants had passed through the door, each of them went into his own room. Egil accompanied Hildir into one and walked in front. As Hildir entered the cave Egil turned on him, got hold of his hair and swung his short-sword, aiming at his throat. But Hildir hit back at him quickly, so Egil was knocked against the rock face, and the skin of his forehead broken. It was quite a big wound and it bled freely, but the short-sword caught the giant's nose and sliced it off. The severed piece was so big, it was a full load for a horse. Hildir managed to get outside and shouted that he had been tricked. The giants inside heard this and made a rush for the exit, but didn't find it easy to get by. At one door Skrogg the Lawman killed everyone who tried to get out and at the other Skin-Beak blinded everyone with the mirror. So the giants ran around to and fro inside the cave, not knowing which way to turn and roaring and banging about.

Gaut heard this and realized what must have happened. When he came to his private cave he saw that the bride was missing, so he rushed over to the bed intending to grab his sword, but found it missing too. Asmund raised the sword and aimed at Gaut, but he didn't take into account how low the ceiling was, so the sword caught the rock and bit through it. But the point of the sword caught Gaut's eye-brow, cut down through the eye, the cheek-bone and collar-bone, and sliced clean through the breast to sever the ribs. Gaut managed to get outside where he picked up a huge boulder and hurled it at Asmund, hitting him in the chest and knocking him down. Gaut made an effort to rush at him but his entrails got tangled up with his feet and he dropped down dead.

Asmund stood up and started looking around for Egil. In the end he came to the place where he and Hildir were fighting it out. Blood was flowing out of Egil's eye from the wound he'd received, and his strength was obviously failing. Asmund caught hold of both Hildir's feet and Egil held on to his head and between them they broke his neck. That was the end of him.

Asmund and Egil went back to Skrogg the Lawman. He'd killed ninety giants, and the rest of them were begging for mercy. The giants who went out through the door guarded by Skin-Beak walked straight over the cliff and killed themselves.

The foster-brothers spent the night in the cave and Eagle-Beak joined them there. In the morning they got hold of all the valuables in the cave and went back home with the old hag. The sisters had already arrived and were delighted to see them. They all stayed there over winter and enjoyed the finest hospitality.

In the spring they got ready to set out and rejoin their own men, but before parting they gave Jotunheim to Eagle-Beak and Skrogg the Lawman. Everyone parted the best of friends. The foster brothers took away with them all the treasures mentioned above. They came to their own men in the last week of winter and there was a happy reunion between them.

As soon as the wind was favourable they put to sea and kept going until they got back to King Hertrygg.

17. ANOTHER WEDDING

King Hertrygg gave them and his daughters a great welcome. They brought him a good many treasures and told him precisely what had happened to them on the trip. The king thanked them handsomely for the journey they had made.

A little later the king called the people to a meeting, and reminded them of the promise he had made to the man who found his daughters. The king asked the foster-brothers whether they'd prefer to get their reward in gold and silver, but both gave the same reply, that they'd rather have his daughters as long as the girls were willing to marry them. The girls knew that the foster-brothers had saved their lives and said they wouldn't want any other men for husbands if they could marry these. So the outcome was that Egil married Bekkhild and Asmund married Brynhild.

The king had preparations made for a wedding feast. Egil said he wanted first to go back home to see if his father was still alive and what his hopes might be concerning the throne, which he thought he had a right to. Asmund said he wanted to go east to Tartary to invite his foster-brother Herraud to the wedding. The time for the wedding was fixed and also the time for their return. There's nothing to say about their travels except that they went well.

When Egil arrived in Gotaland, he went to see his father who completely failed to recognize him, as he thought he must have died a long time before. He told his father in detail what had happened to him (as we've already described it here) and showed the scar on his wrist where his hand had been cut off. He showed him as well the socketed sword the dwarf had made him. They asked the dwarf Regin to fix a handle on it, and after that it was a fine weapon. Egil invited his father, mother and sister to the wedding and when they came to King Hertrygg, Herraud and Asmund had already arrived.

The king gave them all a splendid welcome and it wasn't very long before an excellent feast was in full swing. There were a good many different kinds of musical instruments to be heard there and a good many distinguished people to be seen. No expense had been spared to get the best of everything that could be had in that part of the world.

During the feast Egil and Asmund entertained the guests with stories about their travels, and it's said that to prove the truth of their tale, both Skin-Beak and Eagle-Beak were there and vouched for their story. Queen Ingibjorg recognized Eagle-Beak, and they were completely reconciled.

The feast lasted for a whole month, and when it was over all the guests went back home with splendid gifts. Egil gave Herraud the shirt that Bekkhild had made and Asmund gave him the ring that had belonged to the old hag and the sword as well, that had belonged to Gaut.

King Hertrygg was getting to be an old man, so he asked Egil to stay with him. He said he didn't expect to live much longer. Egil said he wanted first to go home to Gotaland but that he would be back within twelve months. The king gave his permission. Asmund invited Herraud to come with him to Halogaland and Herraud agreed to go.

Eagle-Beak went back home to Jotunheim and Queen Ingibjorg gave her a butter-keg. It was so big she could only just lift it and said they would think it a rare thing in Jotunheim. Asmund gave her two flanks of bacon, so heavy they weighed a ton each. The old hag appreciated these gifts more than if she'd been given a load of gold, and they all parted the best of friends.

18. THE END OF THE STORY

Asmund and Herraud embarked, and sailed off in the fine dragon-headed longship that had belonged to Visin and Bull-Bear. There's nothing to tell of their voyage until they arrived north in Halogaland. When the inhabitants saw their dragon-ship King Ottar remarked that these men must have come a long way.

As soon as they landed, they pitched their tents ashore. Asmund went with eleven men to see his father and greeted him respectfully. The king did not recognize him, but his mother knew him at once and put her arms round him. The king asked who was this stranger his wife was being so friendly to and Asmund gave him the answer. Soon an excellent feast was under way, and they spent a month there enjoying the best of hopsitality. They told the king all about their travels and he thought they'd had plenty of success and good luck.

Herraud told Asmund that he wanted them to go east together to Gotaland to ask for the hand of Æsa, Hring's daughter. Asmund thought this an excellent idea, and as soon as the wind was favourable they sailed east to Gotaland. Egil and Hring gave them a great welcome. Herraud spoke up and asked for Æsa's hand. This was well received and she was given to him with a large dowry. The wedding was celebrated at once and the feast went very well.

After the feast Egil and Herraud sailed to the Baltic, but Asmund stayed behind as he was to become King of Gotaland should Hring die. By the time they got back to Tartary King Hertygg was dead, so Egil was made king, and he and Bekkhild lived there from then on. Herraud took over his own kingdom a little later. Neither of them came north to Scandinavia after that.

Asmund went back home to Halogaland and ruled there for a long time. His son Armod married Edny, daughter of King Hakon Hamundarson of Denmark, and a great progeny has come down from them. This Armod was killed in his bath by Starkad the Old, and that was Starkad's last crime.

Brynhild didn't live long, so Asmund married again. His second wife was the daughter of Sultan, the King of the Saracens. Asmund was supposed to come to the wedding in a single ship, as they intended to trick him. Then Asmund had a ship built that he called the Gnod, the biggest ship that is known to have been built north of the Mediterranean. Because of this ship he was nick-named Gnod-Asmund, and he's considered to have been the greatest of all the ancient kings who did not rule over the major kingdoms.

Asmund was killed near Læso Island and over three thousand men with him. It's said that Odin ran him through with a spear and that Asmund jumped overboard, but the Gnod sank to the bottom with all its cargo and nothing of the ship or the cargo has ever been found.

And so we end this story.

Thorstein Mansion-Might's Story

1. MANSION-MIGHT

About the time Earl Hakon Sigurdarson was ruler of Norway, there was a farmer called Brynjolf Camel living in Gaulardale, a landed man and a great fighter.

Brynjolf was married to Dagny, the daughter of Jarnskeggi of Yrjar, and they had a son called Thorstein; he was a tall strong man, harsh-minded and unflinching, no matter whom he was dealing with. Thorstein was the biggest man in Norway, so big that in the whole country there was hardly a door he could walk through without some difficulty, and since he seemed to be a bit over-developed for most houses he got the name of Thorstein Mansion-Might. Thorstein was so unfriendly, his father gave him a ship with some men and he spent the time alternately plundering or trading, and was equally successful in both.

It was about this time that King Olaf Tryggvason came to the throne of Norway, after Earl Hakon's throat was slit by his own slave Thormod Kark. Thorstein became Olaf's retainer, and the king thought very highly of him for his courage, but the other retainers had no great liking for him. It seemed to them that he was too rough and unyielding. The king used to send Thorstein on dangerous missions that other retainers refused to undertake, but sometimes Thorstein used to go on trading trips to buy things of value for the king.

2. TO THE UNDERWORLD

On one occasion Thorstein was lying off the Finnish coast waiting for a favourable wind. One morning he went ashore, and when the sun was in the south-east he came to a clearing. There was a beautiful mound in the clearing and on top of it stood a bald-headed boy.

'Mother,' he was calling, 'hand me out my crooked stick and gloves, I want to go for a witch-ride. They're having a celebration down below in the Underworld.'

Then a crooked stick, shaped like a poker, was thrown out of the mound. The boy put on the gloves and sat astride the stick and started riding it, as children often do.

Thorstein went up on to the mound and repeated the boy's words. Right away a stick and a pair of gloves were thrown out, and a voice asked,

'Who's wanting these?'

'Your son, Bjalfi,' said Thorstein.

Thorstein got astride the stick and rode after the boy. They came to a wide river and plunged into it and it was as if they were wading through smoke. After some time the mist cleared before their eyes and they came to where the river was cascading over a cliff. Thorstein saw a thickly-populated district and a large town.

They made their way towards the town, and found the people there sitting at table. They walked into the palace where crowds of people were drinking from silver cups. There was a table standing on the floor, and everything seemed to be golden in colour, and nothing was drunk but wine. Then Thorstein realized that they were both invisible to the people there.

The bald-headed boy started along the tables picking up from the floor all the titbits that fell down.

There was a king and a queen sitting on the throne, and all the people inside were enjoying themselves. Then Thorstein saw a man come into the hall and greet the king. The newcomer said he had been sent by the earl who ruled over Mount Lucanus in India, and explained to the king that he was an elf-man. He presented the king with a gold ring. It seemed to the king that he had never seen a more exquisite ring and it was passed around the hall for everyone to admire. This ring could be taken apart in four sections. Thorstein noticed another fine thing that appealed to him very strongly, and that was the cloth on the royal table. It had stripes of gold and was set with twelve precious stones, the best there are. Thorstein had to have the table-cloth, and now it struck him that he might try out King Olaf's luck, and see whether he could get the ring. Now Thorstein saw that the king was about to put the ring on his finger, so he grabbed it and with the other hand took hold of the cloth, spilling all the food into the mud. Then Thorstein ran for the door, leaving the crooked stick behind him.

At once a great uproar broke out; some men ran outside, saw which way he had gone and started after him. He could see now that they might soon catch up with him, so he called out, 'If you are as good, King Olaf, as my faith in you is strong, then help me now.'

Thorstein ran so fast that the pursuers couldn't intercept him until he came to the river and there he had to stop. Then they set on him from all sides, but Thorstein gave a good account of himself, and had killed a number of them when his companion turned up with the crooked stick, and at once they both plunged into the river.

Eventually they got back to the mound they had started from, and now the sun was in the west. The boy threw the stick into the mound and the sack as well, which he had filled with choice food, and Thorstein did the same. The bald-headed boy ran into the mound but Thorstein waited outside at the skylight. He saw two women in the mound, one of them weaving a precious cloth and the other rocking a baby.

The younger one said, 'What can be holding up Bjalfi, your brother?'

'He didn't come with me today,' said the bald-headed boy.

'Who took the crooked stick?' she asked.

'That was Thorstein Mansion-Might,' said Bald-Head, 'King Olaf's retainer. He got us into a lot of trouble by stealing those treasures from the Underworld, the like of which aren't to be found in Norway, and we came very close to being killed when he threw his stick right into their hands. While they were chasing him to his death I brought the stick back to him. He's certainly a very brave man and I've no idea how many he may have killed.' With that the mound closed.

Thorsten went back to his men, and sailed off to Norway. He found King Olaf in Oslofjord, gave him the treasures and told the story of his travels, which made a great impression on everyone. The king offered to give Thorstein big estates, but he said he wanted to take one more trip to the east. Then he stayed with the king over winter.

3. THE DWARF

In the spring Thorstein made his ship ready and gathered a crew of twenty-four men. He sailed first to Jamtland, and one day when he was lying in harbour there he went ashore for a stroll. He came to a clearing and saw a hideous-looking dwarf standing there beside a huge boulder, screaming at the top of his voice. It seemed to Thorstein as if the dwarf's mouth was twisted up to the ear on one side, and on the other side the nose overlapped the mouth. Thorstein asked the dwarf why he was acting like a madman.

'And no wonder, man!' said the dwarf. 'Can't you see that great eagle flying over there? It's got hold of my son. It must be a devil sent by Odin himself. It'll kill me if I lose that child.'

Thorstein aimed a shot at the eagle, hitting it under the wings, and the bird dropped down dead. Thorstein caught the dwarf's boy as he fell and gave him back to his father. The dwarf was very happy and said, 'My son and I owe you a great debt for saving his life, and now I'd like you to choose your own reward in gold and silver.'

'You'd better see to your son first,' said Thorstein, 'and anyway, I'm not in the habit of taking money just for showing my strength.'

'That doesn't make my duty to repay you any the less,' said the dwarf, 'I don't suppose you'd consider accepting my sheep's wool shirt? You'll never get tired at swimming and never be wounded as long as your wear it next to your skin.'

Thorstein tried on the shirt and it was a perfect fit although it had seemed too small for the dwarf. He also took a silver ring from his purse and gave it to Thorstein, warning him to take good care of it, for he would never be short of money as long as he kept the ring.

Then the dwarf gave Thorstein a black flint. 'If you hide this in the palm of your hand no one can see you. There aren't any other useful things I can give you, except for a bit of marble I want you to have just for your amusement.'

He took this bit of marble from his purse and with it a steel point. The marble was triangular in shape, white in the centre and one of the sides was red, with a yellow ring around it.

The dwarf said, 'If you prick the white part with the point, a hail-storm will come, so fierce that no one will be able to face it. When you want to thaw out the snow, you have only to prick the yellow part and the sun will shine and melt it all away. But when you prick the red part, fire and flames with a shower of sparks will come flying out of it so that no one will be able to bear it. Besides that you can hit anything you aim at with the point and the marble, and they'll both come back into your hands when you call for them. This, then, is all the reward I can give you for the time being.'

Thorstein thanked him for the gifts and went back to his men, feeling that this trip had not been altogether wasted. Then they got a favourable wind and sailed on to the East, but soon they ran into fogs and lost their bearings. For a whole fortnight they had no idea where they were going.

4. GIANTLAND

One evening they realized that they were close to land, so they cast anchor and lay there overnight. In the morning the weather was fine, with bright sunshine. They saw that they were in a long narrow fjord, with lovely wooded slopes on either side. No one on board could identify this land. They could see no living thing anywhere, neither beast nor bird. So they set up their tents ashore and made themselves comfortable.

The following morning Thorstein said to his men, 'I want to let you know what I have in mind. You're to wait for me here for six days while I go and explore this land.'

They weren't at all happy about this and insisted on going with him, but Thorstein wouldn't have it. 'If I don't come back before the seventh sunset,' he said, 'you're to sail back home and tell King Olaf that it's not my fate ever to return.'

They walked with him as far as the wood and then he vanished out of sight. They made their way back to the ship and waited there as he had told them to.

Thorstein walked on through the forest all day without noticing anything particular, but towards evening he came to a wide road and followed it till dusk. Then he turned off the road and made for a huge oak tree. He climbed it and found there was plenty of room to lie down, so he slept there through the night.

At sunrise he heard a great deal of noise and some voices speaking and saw twenty-two men riding hard past the tree. Thorstein was amazed to see how big they were – he had never seen such huge men as these before. He put on his clothes, and the morning passed till the sun was in the south-east.

5. GODMUND OF GLASIR PLAINS

Then Thorstein saw three horsemen riding up, fully armed and so enormous, he had never seen such men. The one in the middle was the tallest, and was wearing gold-trimmed clothes and riding a pale-dun horse. His two companions wore scarlet clothing and rode on grey horses.

When they came opposite the tree where Thorstein was hiding the leader said, 'What's that moving in the oak?'

Thorstein climbed down to meet them and when he greeted them they all burst out laughing. The tall man said, 'It's not every day that we see someone like you. What's your name, and where are you from?'

Thorstein gave his name, and added that he was also known as Mansion-Might. 'My family belongs to Norway, and I'm King Olaf's man.'

The tall man smiled and said, 'This regal splendour of his must be a great lie, if he has nobody braver-looking than you. In my opinion you ought to be called Mansion-Midget, not Mansion-Might.'

'Give me a naming-gift, then,' said Thorstein.

The tall man took a gold ring off his finger and gave it to Thorstein.

'What name do you have?' asked Thorstein, 'What's your background, and what's the name of this country?'

'I'm called Godmund, and I'm the ruler of Glasir Plains; this country's a dependency of Giantland. I'm a king's son, and these are my companions, Full-Strong and All-Strong. Did you by any chance see some riders pass by this morning?'

'Twenty-two men rode past here,' said Thorstein, 'and they weren't exactly unobtrusive.'

'Those would have been my lads,' said Godmund. 'The neighbouring country's called Jotunheim and there's a King called Geirrod ruling it just now. We're tributaries under him. My father, Ulfhedin Trusty, was known as Godmund, as all the other rulers of Glasir Plains have been. He travelled over to Geirrod's town to hand over his tribute to the king, but during this trip my father died, so King Geirrod has asked me to a funeral feast in my father's honour, and to take my father's titles as well. But we're not happy about being ruled by giants.'

'Why did your men ride ahead of you?' asked Thorstein.

'There's a great river that divides our countries. It's known as the Hemra and it's so deep and swift that the only horses that can ford it are the three we're riding on. The rest of my men have to ride as far as the source of the river, but we'll all meet tonight.'

'It could be amusing to go with you and see what happens there,' said Thorstein.

'I'm not so sure about that,' said Godmund, 'I suppose you're a Christian.'

'I can take care of myself,' said Thorstein.

'I shouldn't want you to come to any harm on my account,' said Godmund. 'But if King Olaf will give us his good luck, I'm willing to risk taking you with us.'

Thorstein gave his word, so Godmund told Thorstein to get up behind him, which is what he did.

They rode as far as the river. On the bank there was a hut and from it they took a set of clothes for themselves and their horses. These clothes were made so that the water couldn't touch them, but the river was so cold that it would cause instant gangrene to any part of the body that came into contact with the water. They forded the river, with the horses struggling hard, but Godmund's horse stumbled, so Thorstein got his toe wet, and gangrene set in at once. When they got out of the river they spread their clothes on the ground to dry. Thorstein cut off his toe, and they were immensely impressed by his toughness. So they rode on their way.

Thorstein told them there was no need for them to hide him. 'I can make myself a helmet of invisibility, so nobody can see me,' he added. Godmund said this was a useful skill to have. When they arrived at Geirrodstown, Godmund's men came to meet them, so they rode all together into the town. They could hear the music of all kinds of instruments, but Thorstein didn't think much of the tune. King Geirrod came out to meet them and gave them a good welcome. They were

I

shown to a stone-house or hall where they were suppsed to sleep and their horses were taken to the stable.

Godmund was escorted into the royal palace where the king was sitting on the throne and beside him Earl Agdi, ruler of Grundir which lies between Giantland and Jotunheim. Agdi had his residence at a place called Gripalund; he was a sorcerer and his men were more like giant trolls than human beings.

Godmund sat down on a footstool beside the highseat opposite the king. It was their custom that no prince could take his seat on the throne until he had assumed his father's titles and the first toast had been drunk.

Soon an excellent feast was well under way, with everyone drinking and having a good time. When it was over the guests went to sleep, and as soon as Godmund came back to his quarters Thorstein made himself visible. They all laughed at him until Godmund told them who he was and asked them not to make fun of him.

So they slept soundly through the night.

6. DRINKING

Early in the morning they were all up, and Godmund was led to the royal palace. The king gave him a good welcome. 'What I'd like to know now,' he said, 'is whether you're willing to show me the same obedience as your father did. If so, I'm willing to add to your titles and let you keep Giantland as long as you swear me an oath of loyalty.'

Godmund answered, 'That isn't lawful, to demand oaths of a man as young as me.'

'Have it your way,' said the king.

Then he took a cloak of precious material and laid it over Godmund and gave him the title of King. Geirrod picked up a large drinking horn and gave a toast to Godmund, who took the horn and thanked the king. Then Godmund stood up and stepped on to the foot-board in front of the high-seat before the king and made a solemn vow that he would neither serve nor obey any other king as long as Geirrod lived. The king thanked him for that and said it pleased him more than if he had sworn him formal oaths. Then Godmund emptied the horn and returned to his seat. Everyone was cheerful and happy.

Earl Agdi had two men with him, called Jokul and Frosti, both very jealous men. Jokul now took hold of an ox-bone and hurled it at Godmund's men. Thorstein saw this, caught it in flight, and sent it back where it came from, hitting a man called Gust right in the face, breaking his nose and every tooth in his mouth, and knocking him senseless.

This infuriated King Geirrod and he asked who were hurling bones over his table, adding that before it was all over they would find out which of them had the strongest throwing-arm.

Then King Geirrod called over two men, Drott and Hosvir:

'Go and fetch my gold ball, and bring it here,' he told them.

Off they went, and came back with a seal's head weighing two hundred pounds. It was red-hot, with sparks flashing from it like a forge-fire and the fat was dripping from it like burning tar.

The king said, 'Take the ball now and throw it at each other. Anyone who drops it will be made an outlaw and forfeit all his property: and anybody who's afraid to throw the ball, he'll be marked out as an utter coward.'

7. THE BALL-GAME

Now Drott hurled the ball at Full-Strong who caught it with one hand, but Thorstein realized that Full-Strong's strength was not quite sufficient so he flung himself against the ball. Together they threw the ball at Frosti, because all the champions were standing in front of the benches on either side. Frosti caught the ball with firm hands but it went so close to his face that the cheek-bone was broken. He threw the ball back at All-Strong who caught it with both hands, but his knee would have given way had Thorstein not supported him.

All-Strong hurled the ball at Earl Agdi who caught it with both hands, but the burning fat from the ball splashed on to his beard, setting it all on fire. So he was in a hurry to get rid of the ball and hurled it at King Godmund, who threw it at King Geirrod, but he dodged out of the way so the ball hit Drott and Hosvir, killing them both. The ball travelled on through a glass window and crashed into the moat that

surrounded the town, and flames erupted from it. And that was the end
of the game. Earl Agdi said he felt shivers down the spine every time
he came anywhere near Godmund's men.

In the evening Godmund and his men went to sleep. They thanked
Thorstein for all his help and protection from danger. He told them not
to mention it – 'but what sort of entertainment can we expect tomorrow?'

'The King will make us wrestle,' said Godmund. 'They'll try to get
their own back on us, since they're much stronger than we are.'

'King Olaf's luck will strengthen us,' said Thorstein. 'Don't forget,
let the scuffle take you over to where I am.'

So they slept through the night.

In the morning everyone went to his own favourite kind of entertainment while the servants were laying the tables. King Geirrod asked the
guests whether they wouldn't like to wrestle, and they said they would
if that was what he wanted. So they stripped and the wrestling match
began. It seemed to Thorstein that he'd never seen such a clash because
whenever someone was thrown the whole place shook. It was obvious
that Earl Agdi's men were losing the contest.

Frosti stepped on to the floor and said, 'Who's going to take me
on?'

'I daresay someone will,' said Full-Strong.

They set about each other and there was a fierce struggle between
them. Frosti was much the stronger, and the scuffle took them to
Godmund's place. Frosti heaved Full-Strong up to his chest, but had to
bend his knees. Then Thorstein kicked him behind the knees so Frosti
fell flat on his back with Full-Strong on top. The back of Frosti's head
was broken, and so were his elbows.

He got slowly to his feet and said, 'You're not playing singles in this
game. And what makes you smell so foul?'

'Your nose is too close to your own mouth,' said Full-Strong.

Now Jokul got up and All-Strong turned on him. Their clash was
the hardest yet, but Jokul seemed the more powerful and dragged All-
Strong to the bench where Thorstein was. Then Jokul tried hard to
force All-Strong away from there, but Thorstein held on to him. Jokul
pulled so hard that his feet sank into the floor, ankle-deep, and then

Thorstein suddenly pushed All-Strong away from him, so Jokul fell flat on his back and dislocated his leg.

All-Strong went back to his seat, but Jokul got slowly to his feet and said, 'We can't see all those who're on that bench.'

Geirrod asked Godmund whether he wouldn't join in the wrestling, and Godmund said that although he'd never wrestled before he wouldn't turn down the offer. The King ordered Earl Agdi to avenge his men, and he replied that although he'd given up wrestling long ago, he would do what the King wanted.

So they stripped off their clothes. Thorstein thought he had never seen a body more inhuman than Agdi's, for it was black as death. Godmund rose to his feet to meet him, and his skin was very white. Earl Agdi went for him in a rage, and clutched at Godmund's ribs so hard he went right though to the bone. They staggered about all over the hall and when they came to Thorstein, Godmund tried to put down the earl with a hip-throw and swung him hard around. Thorstein threw himself under the earl's feet, toppling him over so he crashed on his nose. He broke not only his thieving nose but four teeth as well. The earl stood up and said, 'An old man always takes a heavy fall, particularly when he's got three against him.'

So they put their clothes on again.

8. MORE DRINKING

After this the king and his guests sat down at table. Earl Agdi and the others said they must have been tricked in some way. 'I always feel hot under the collar whenever I meet up with that crowd.'

'Leave it be,' said the king, 'someone will turn up to make us wiser.'

Then the drinking began, and two horns were carried into the hall. They belonged to Earl Agdi and were great treasures. The horns were called the Whitings, and were two yards long and all inlaid with gold.

The king sent one horn to either side. 'Each man's to empty the horn in one go and anybody who can't manage it shall pay the steward an ounce of silver.'

Only the champions could drink it up in one draught, but Thorstein saw to it that none of Godmund's men was penalized. When this was over, the drinking continued in a lighter mood for the rest of the day; and in the evening the men went to sleep.

Godmund thanked Thorstein for all his help, and Thorstein asked him when the feast would be over.

'My men have to leave in the morning,' said Godmund. 'I know the king will try to get his own back when he shows off his treasures. He'll have his great drinking horn brought into the hall. It's called Grim the Good, and it's a magnificent treasure, ornamented with gold and magical too. There's a man's head on the narrow point, with flesh and mouth, and it can talk to people and tell them what the future holds for them and warn them when there's trouble ahead. It will be the death of us all if the king finds out that we've had a Christian with us. We'll have to be very generous to Grim.'

Thorstein said that Grim wouldn't be able to say any more than King Olaf would let him. 'I think Geirrod's a doomed man. If you'll take my advice, you'll do as I tell you from now on. Tomorrow I'm going to show myself.'

They said it would be a terrible risk, but Thorstein replied that Geirrod wanted them all out of the way. 'What else can you tell me about Grim the Good?' he asked.

'First, that the horn is so long, an average man can stand upright in the curve. The ornamental rim round the opening is a yard wide and while their greatest drinker can drink so deep into the horn, only the king can finish it all in one go. Everybody is supposed to give Grim something valuable, but the greatest honour you can show him is to empty the horn in one go. I know I'm supposed to be the first to drink from the horn, but there isn't a mortal man tough enough to finish it off in one.'

Thorstein said, 'You'd better put on my shirt, because if you do, nothing can harm you, not even poison in the drink. Take the crown off your head, give it to Grim the Good and whisper into his ear that you'll give him much greater honour than Geirrod does, and then you're to pretend to be drinking. But since there's going to be poison in the horn, you'd better pour the drink under your clothes, and then it won't hurt you. But when all the drinking is over you'd better arrange for your men to ride away.'

Godmund told him to have it his way. 'If Geirrod dies, the whole of Jotunheim belongs to me, but if he lives much longer, we're sure to be killed.'

So they slept through the night.

9. GRIM THE GOOD

In the morning they were up early and dressed. Then King Geirrod came and asked them to drink his health, which they did. First they drank from the Whitings and then from the loving-cups. After that the toasts dedicated to Thor and Odin were drunk. Then a number of musical instruments all came playing into the hall, and two men, both rather smaller than Thorstein, carried in Grim the Good between them. All the people got to their feet, then knelt down before him, but there was an ugly look about Grim.

Geirrod spoke to Godmund, 'Take Grim the Good and let this toast bind you to your pledge.'

Godmund went over to Grim, took his gold crown off, put it on Grim's head, and whispered into his ear as Thorstein had instructed him. Next, he poured the poisonous drink into his shirt. When he had drunk in this way to King Geirrod's health, he kissed the point of the horn and Grim was taken away from him with a smile on his face.

Geirrod took the full horn and asked Grim to bring him good luck and warn him if there was any danger about. 'I've often seen you in a happier mood,' he said.

He took a gold necklace he was wearing and gave it to Grim, and then he drank a toast to Earl Agdi. It was like a wave crashing over a skerry when the drink cascaded down his throat. He drank it all up, but Grim only shook his head. Then the horn was carried over to Earl Agdi who gave Grim two gold bracelets and asked him for mercy. He drank it up in three draughts and handed the horn back to the cup-bearer.

Grim said, 'The older a man gets, the feebler he becomes.'

Then the horn was filled yet again, and this time Jokul and Full-Strong were to drink from it. Full-Strong was the first to drink. Jokul took it from him, looked into it and said he had drunk very feebly, then struck at Full-Strong with the horn. But he hit back and drove his fist against Jokul's nose, breaking his thievish chin, and scattering his teeth. This caused a great uproar. Geirrod told them not to let it be put about that they'd parted on such bad terms. So they were reconciled and Grim the Good was borne out.

10. GEIRROD'S DEATH

A little later a man came walking into the hall. Everyone was amazed to see how tiny he was, but this was Thorstein Mansion-Midget. He turned to Godmund and told him that his horses were ready now. Geirrod asked who that little child was.

Godmund said, 'This is my servant-boy that Odin sent me. He's a real king's treasure and knows a trick or two. If you think you could use him I'm willing to give him to you.'

'He seems a striking little lad,' said the king. 'I'd like to see him in action.' He asked Thorstein to perform some trick or other.

Thorstein took his marble and point and started pricking the white part. Then there was such a terrifying hail-storm that no one dared open his eyes, and snow piled up in the hall ankle-deep. This made the king laugh. Then Thorstein pricked the yellow part of the marble, and blazing-hot sunshine burst out over the hall, thawing all the snow in a moment. With this came a sweet fragrance and the king said that Thorstein was indeed a man of extraordinary skill.

Thorstein said he had still one more trick up his sleeve and that one was called the *Scourge*. The king wanted to see it. So Thorstein stepped into the middle of the floor and pricked the red part of the marble. Sparks started flashing from it, and Thorstein ran all over the hall to every seat, with more and more sparks flying from the marble, so that everyone had to cover his eyes; but King Geirrod only laughed at this. The fires increased until everyone felt that it was getting beyond a joke. Thorstein had warned Godmund beforehand that this was the time for him to go outside and get away on horseback.

Thorstein ran up to Geirrod and asked, 'Do you still want more of this game?'

'Yes, let me see more, my boy,' he said.

So Thorstein pricked still harder than ever and the sparks got into Geirrod's eyes. Thorstein rushed to the door, and threw the marble and point straight into Geirrod's eyes, knocking him down dead on to the floor. When Thorstein got outside Godmund had already mounted.

Thorstein said they must ride off at once. 'This is no place for weaklings any longer,' he said.

They rode over to the river and by that time the marble and point had come back. Thorstein told them that Geirrod was dead. So they forded the river and rode on to the spot where Thorstein had first met them.

Thorstein said, 'We'd better part now; my men will be thinking it's time for me to join them.'

'Come home with me,' said Godmund, 'I'll repay all the help you've given us.'

'I'll come for that some other time,' said Thorstein. 'But you'd better go back to Geirrodstown with plenty of men. You can get control of the whole country now.'

'Whatever you say,' said Godmund. 'Give King Olaf my regards.'

Then he handed Thorstein a gold bowl, a silver dish and a gold-embroidered towel to take to King Olaf. Godmund asked Thorstein to come and visit him, and they parted the best of friends.

11. BACK TO NORWAY

Next Thorstein caught sight of Earl Agdi who was storming along in a gigantic fury. Thorstein followed him until they came to the large farmstead where Agdi lived. There was a young woman standing at the gate to the orchard – Agdi's daughter. Her name was Gudrun, and she was a tall, good-looking girl. She greeted her father and asked him the news.

'There's news enough,' he said. 'King Geirrod's dead. Godmund of Glasir Plain has tricked us all and hidden a Christian there called Thorstein Mansion-Midget. He's thrown fire into our eyes, but now I'm on my way to kill his men.'

Earl Agdi threw down the Whitings and ran into the wood as if he were out of his mind.

Thorstein went up to Gudrun. She greeted him and asked him his name and he told her he was called Thorstein Mansion-Midget, one of King Olaf's men.

'His biggest must be very big indeed, if you're the midget,' she said.

'Will you come with me and embrace our faith?' said Thorstein.

'There's not much here to keep me happy,' she said. 'My mother's dead. She was the daughter of Earl Ottar of Novgorod, and she wasn't a bit like my father in temperament, because he's very much the giant. I can see now that he's doomed, so if you promise to bring me back here, I'll go with you.'

She collected her things, and Thorstein took the Whitings. They went into the wood and saw Agdi going about screaming, with his hands over his eyes. Two things had happened simultaneously; as he caught sight of Thorstein's ship he felt a terrible pain in his thief's eyes and went blind.

It was sunset by the time Thorstein and Gudrun reached the ship and his men were ready to sail. But when they saw Thorstein, they were delighted. He stepped on board and right away they put to sea.

There is nothing to tell of his voyage till he arrived home in Norway.

12. THE WEDDING

That winter King Olaf was in residence at Trondheim, and Thorstein went to see him at Christmas to bring him the gifts which Godmund had sent him and also the Whitings and many other valuable things besides.

Thorstein told the king about his travels and introduced Gudrun to him. The king thanked him warmly and everyone was very impressed and praised his courage. The king had Gudrun baptized and instructed in the Christian faith. At Christmas Thorstein played the *Scourge* and everyone thought it great entertainment. The Whitings were used when toasts were being drunk, with two men sharing each horn. The loving-cup Godmund had sent the king was so big that no one could drink from it except Thorstein Mansion-Midget. The towel wouldn't burn even when it was thrown on the fire: the flames only made it cleaner than before.

Thorstein mentioned to the king that he intended to marry Gudrun. The king gave his consent and there was a splendid feast. On their wedding-night when they had just gone to bed, the curtain came crashing down, the panelling over Thorstein's head burst open, and through it appeared Earl Agdi with the idea of killing Thorstein. But he was hit by such a wave of hot air he didn't dare go inside. Then King Olaf came and thumped Agdi's head with a gold-trimmed staff, hammering him right into the ground. After that, the king kept watch throughout the night.

In the morning the Whitings had vanished, but the wedding-feast went ahead without a hitch. Thorstein stayed over winter with the king and he and Gudrun loved each other dearly.

In the spring Thorstein asked permission to sail to the east to see King Godmund. But King Olaf said he couldn't go unless he promised to come back, so Thorstein gave his word. The king asked him to keep his faith well, 'And put more trust in yourself than in those people to the east,' he added.

They parted the best of friends, and everyone wished Thorstein good luck, as he had now become a very popular man. So he sailed to the Baltic, and as far as is known the voyage went smoothly for him. He arrived finally at Glasir Plains and Godmund gave him a good welcome.

Thorstein said, 'Have you heard anything from Geirrodstown?'

'I went there myself,' said Godmund, 'and they surrendered the country into my power. My son Heidrek Wolf-Skin's ruling over it.'

'What happened to Earl Agdi?' said Thorstein.

'After you left Agdi had a burial mound built for himself,' said Godmund, 'and then he retired into it with a great deal of money. Jokul and Frosti were drowned in the river Hemra, on their way back home from the feast, so now I'm in full control of the district of Grundir as well.'

'What matters to me,' said Thorstein, 'is how much of it you're prepared to let me have, since it seems to me my wife's entitled to all the inheritance after her father, Earl Agdi.'

'You can have it all if you become my man,' said Godmund.

'Then you won't interfere with my faith?' said Thorstein.

'That's a promise,' said Godmund.

So they went to the district of Grundir and Thorstein took charge of it.

13. THE END

Thorstein rebuilt the house at Gripalund as Earl Agdi had come back from the dead and destroyed the old home. Thorstein became a great chieftain, and a little later Gudrun gave birth to a fine big boy who was called Brynjolf.

Earl Agdi couldn't restrain himself from playing tricks on Thorstein. One night Thorstein got out of bed and saw Agdi wandering about, but Agdi didn't dare go through any of the gates as there was a cross on every one of them. So Thorstein went over to his mound. It was open, so he went inside and picked up the Whitings. Then Agdi came into the mound, and Thorstein ran out past him and put a cross in the doorway. The mound closed up, and since then nothing has ever been seen of Agdi.

Next summer Thorstein went back to Norway and gave King Olaf the Whitings. Then he got permission to go back to his own possessions. The king told him he should keep his faith well. Since then we have not heard anything about Thorstein, but when King Olaf disappeared from the Long Serpent the Whitings vanished, and so we end the story of Thorstein Mansion-Midget.

Helgi Thorisson's Story

1. THE WOMAN

There was a man called Thorir farming at Raudaberg near Oslofjord in
Norway. He had two sons, Helgi and Thorstein, both fine men, though
Helgi was the more talented of the two. Their father was a man of some
rank and enjoyed the friendship of King Olaf Tryggvason.

One summer the brothers went on a trading voyage north to Finnmark, with butter and bacon to sell to the Laps. Their trade went very
successfully, and late in the summer they sailed back south again. One
day they came to the headland called Vimund where there are fine
woods. They went ashore and cut themselves a certain maple tree.
Helgi happened to stroll deeper into the wood than the rest of his men.
Suddenly a heavy mist came down over the forest, so that he couldn't
find his way back to the ship that same evening, and soon night fell and
it grew very dark.

Then Helgi saw twelve women come riding through the wood, all of
them on red-coloured horses and wearing red costumes. They dis-
mounted, and all their riding-gear shone with gold. One woman was
far lovelier than all the others, and they were in attendance upon this
distinguished woman.

They put out their horses to graze, then the women set up a splendid
tent, with stripes of alternating colours and embroidered everywhere
with gold. The points of the tent were ornamented with gold, and on
top of the pole which stood up through the tent there was a great golden
ball. When the women had made these preparations, they set up a table
and laid it with all kinds of choice food. Then they took water to wash
their hands, using a jug and basins of silver, inlaid everywhere with
gold.

Helgi was standing near the tent watching them, and the distinguished
woman said to him, 'Come over here, Helgi, have something to eat and
drink with us.'

So that's what he did, and he could see that the food and wine were
delicious, and the cups quite splendid. When the table had been cleared,
the beds were made – these beds were much more ornate than those of

other people – the distinguished woman asked Helgi whether he would prefer to sleep alone or share a bed with her. He asked her name.

'I'm called Ingibjorg. I'm the daughter of Godmund of Glasir Plains,' she said.

'I'd like to sleep with you,' he said.

So they slept together for three successive nights.

On the third morning the weather was fine, so they got up and dressed.

'This is where we part company,' she said. 'There are two boxes here, one full of silver, the other of gold. I'm going to give you these, but you must on no account tell anyone where you got them.'

Then the women rode off the same way as they had come, and Helgi went back to the ship. They gave him a great welcome and asked him where he'd been, but he wouldn't tell.

They sailed on south along the coast until they came home to their father with plenty of money. Helgi's father and brother wanted to know where he'd got all this money in the boxes, but he wouldn't say anything about it.

2. THE STRANGERS

So time passed till Christmas, and then one night a terrible gale sprang up. Thorstein said to his brother:

'We'd better get up and see what's happening to our ship.'

So that's what they did, and saw the ship was secure.

Helgi had had a dragon-head fitted on to their ship's prow, and the whole stem was decorated above the sea-line. This is how Helgi had invested part of the money Ingibjorg had given him, but some of it he'd locked in the neck of the dragon.

The brothers heard a terrific crash, then two riders suddenly appeared and carried Helgi off with them. Thorstein had no idea what could have happened to him. When the weather cleared up again, Thorstein went back home to tell his father what had happened, and everybody thought it terrible news.

Helgi's father went at once to see King Olaf, told him all about it and asked him to find out what had happened to his son. The king said he'd

do as Thorir wanted but added that he very much doubted if Helgi
would ever be much use to his family again. After that, Thorir went
back home.

The year went by, till it was Christmas again. That winter, King
Olaf was in residence at Alreksstead. On the eighth day of Christmas,
in the evening, three strangers came into the hall before King Olaf as he
was sitting at table. They greeted him respectfully, and the king returned their greetings. One of these men was Helgi, but no one
recognized the other two.

The king asked them their names, and each said he was called Grim.
'We've been sent to you by Godmund of Glasir Plains,' they said. 'He
sends you his compliments and also these two drinking horns.'

The king accepted the horns. Precious things they were, all inlaid
with gold. King Olaf owned two other drinking horns, called the
Hyrnings and thought to be great treasures, but the horns from Godmund were far better than these.

'What King Godmund wants, my lord, is for you to be his friend.
He sets a higher value on your friendship than that of any other king,'
they said.

The king didn't answer that, but had them shown back to their seats.
The king had the two horns (these incidentally were also both called
Grim), filled with good ale and after that, had them blessed by a bishop.
Then the king had the horns called Grim brought first to the two men
called Grim, so they could take the first draught.

King Olaf said:

'Our guests must take
these drinking horns,
while we give rest
to Godmund's men.
The Grims must drink
from their namesakes,
and see how good
our ale can be.'

The two Grims took the horns and now they realized what the bishop
must have sung over the drink.

K

'It's just as our King Godmund told us,' they said. 'This king's full of tricks, he exchanges evil for good, while our king treats him with the greatest honour. Let's stand up and get out of here.'

And that's what they did, which caused a great stir in the hall, as they spilled the drink and put all the lights out. Then everybody heard a great crashing sound. The king prayed for God's protection, and told his men to get up and put an end to the noise, but by this time the two Grims and Helgi had got outside. When the lights were relit in the king's hall, they saw three men had been killed and the Grim-horns lying beside their bodies.

'This is an extraordinary thing to happen,' said the king. 'Let's hope it doesn't happen too often. People tell me Godmund of Glasir Plains is a great sorcerer and a bad man to have as an enemy. It's no joke for anyone to get into his power, even if we could do something about it.' Then the king told his men to take care of the horns and carry on drinking from them, and they gave no trouble to anyone.

The mountain pass the two Grims had travelled through on their way west down to Alreksstead is now known as Grim Pass and no one has ever used that route since.

3. THE VICTIM

Winter passed, and then the year, till it was the eighth day of Christmas once more, and the king was in church with his retainers attending Mass. Then three men came up to the church door, and one of them stayed on, but the other two went away again. This is what they said before they left – 'We've brought a skeleton for your feast, my lord, and you'll not so easily get rid of it again.'

The retainers saw that this man was Helgi. When the king went to eat and his men tried to talk to Helgi, they realized he was blind. The king asked how things were with him and where he had been all this time. Helgi told him the whole story, how he'd met the women in the wood. How the Grims had brought the gale on him and his brother when they were trying to save their ship, and how the Grims had finally brought him to Godmund of Glasir Plains and handed him over to Ingibjorg, Godmund's daughter.

'How did you like it there?' asked the king.

'Pretty well,' he said. 'There's nowhere I've liked better.'

Then the king asked him about the way King Godmund lived, how many men he had, and what kind of things he did. Helgi spoke very highly of everything and answered that there was much more to be said about King Godmund than he could ever tell them.

'Why did you clear off in such a hurry last winter?' said the king.

'King Godmund sent the two Grims to fool you,' said Helgi, 'and he only let me go because of your prayers, so that you could learn what had happened to me. The reason we left in such a hurry last year was that the Grims weren't able to drink the ale when you'd had it blessed. It got them into a rage to be beaten like that. They killed your men because that's what Godmund had told them to, if they couldn't harm you personally. But he sent you the horns just to make an impression, and to take your mind off me.'

'Why did you go away this time?' asked the king.

'Because of Ingibjorg,' said Helgi. 'She said she couldn't sleep with me without feeling uneasy whenever she touched my naked body, that's mainly why I had to leave. In the long run, King Godmund didn't want to argue when he realized you were so keen to get me away from there. As for King Godmund's splendour and generosity, I haven't the words to describe it, nor the great numbers he had with him.'

'Why are you blind?' asked the king.

'Ingibjorg gouged out both my eyes when we parted,' said Helgi. 'She said the women in Norway wouldn't enjoy my company for very long.'

'Godmund needs to be taught a real lesson for all those killings of his – God willing,' said the king.

Then Helgi's father, Thorir, was sent for, and he couldn't thank Olaf enough for getting his son out of those monsters' hands. Thorir went back home, but Helgi stayed on with the king and lived for exactly one more year.

King Olaf took the Grim-horns with him when he set out on his last journey. It's said that when King Olaf disappeared from the Long Serpent, the horns vanished too, and no one has ever seen them since. And this is the last we can tell you about the Grims.

LIST OF PROPER NAMES

The following abbreviations are used: *Gautr* (Gautrek's Saga), *EA* (Egil and Asmund), *BH* (Bosi and Herraud), *Thorst* (Thorstein Mansion-Might's Story), and *HTh* (Helgi Thorisson's Story). The numbers refer to chapters, not pages.

PERSONAL NAMES

ÆLLA, king of England, *Gautr*, 9–11.
ÆSA, sister of Egil One-Hand, *EA*, 9, 18.
AGDI, earl of Grundir, *Thorst*, 5, 7–9, 11–13.
AGNAR, king of Noatown, *BH*, 2.
AGNI, father of Eirik and Alrek, *Gautr*, 7.
ALF, king of Alfheim, *Gautr*, 3.
ALFHILD, grandmother of Starkad, *Gautr*, 3, 7.
ALFHILD, wife of Gautrek, *Gautr*, 8.
ALL-STRONG (Allsterkr), one of King Godmund's men, *Thorst*, 5, 7.
ALREK, king of Sweden, *Gautr*, 7.
AN, one of Vikar's men, *Gautr*, 4.
ARAN, son of King Rodian, *EA*, 6–8.
ARMOD, son of Asmund Berserks-Killer, *EA*, 18.
ASMUND BERSERKS-KILLER, son of King Ottar, *EA*, passim.
BEKKHILD, daughter of King Hertrygg, *EA*, 2, 14, 15, 17.
BJALFI, an alias for Thorstein, *Thorst* 2.
BJARKMAR, earl of Gotaland, *EA*, 9, 12.
BORGAR, a Viking leader, *EA*, 10.
BOSI (STUNT-BOSI), son of a retired Viking, *BH*, passim.
BRYNHILD, daughter of King Hertrygg, *EA*, 1 (14), 15, 17.
BRYNHILD (STUNT-BRYNHILD), mother of Bosi, *BH*, 2.
BRYN-THVARI, *see* THVARI.
BRYNJOLF, son of Thorstein Mansion-Might, *Thorst*, 13.
BRYNJOLF CAMEL (B. Úlfaldi), father of Thorstein Mansion-Might, *Thorst*, 1.
BULL-BEAR (Bola-björn), son of Earl Gorm, *EA*, 7, 17.

BUSLA, fostermother of Bosi, *BH*, 2, 4, 5, 14.

DAGNY, mother of Thorstein Mansion-Might, *Thorst*, 1.

DAYFARER (Dagfari), one of King Harald Wartooth's men, *BH*, 1, 9.

DROTT, one of King Geirrod's men, *Thorst*, 6–7.

DUMB, king of the Dumb Sea, *EA*, 15.

EAGLE-BEAK (Arinnefja), queen of Jotunheim, *EA*, 5, 15–17.

EDDA, daughter of King Harek, *BH*, 7, 13, 16.

EDNY, daughter of King Hakon, *EA*, 18.

EGIL ONE-HAND, son of King Hring of the Smalands, *EA*, passim.

EIRIK, king of Sweden, *Gautr*, 7.

ERP, one of Vikar's men, *Gautr*, 4, 5.

'FJALAR', Egil One-Hand in disguise, *EA*, 15.

FJOLMOD, one of the backwoodsmen, *Gautr*, 1–2.

FJORI, son of Earl Freki, *Gautr*, 3.

FJOTRA, sister and wife of Imsigull, *Gautr*, 1–2.

FREKI, earl of Halogaland, *Gautr*, 3.

FREYJA, the goddess, *BH*, 12.

FRITHJOF THE BRAVE, the eponymous hero of one of the legendary sagas, *Gautr*, 3.

FRITHJOF, king of Telemark, *Gautr*, 3, 5.

FROSTI, one of earl Agdi's men, *Thorst*, 6–7.

'FROSTI', Asmund Berserks-Killer in disguise, *EA*, 15.

FULL-STRONG (Fullsterkr), one of King Godmund's men, *Thorst*, 6, 9.

FYRI, son of Earl Freki, *Gautr*, 3.

GAUT, uncle of Queen Eagle-Beak, *EA*, 12, 14–15.

GAUTI, son of King Odin; grandfather of Herraud; king of West-Gotaland, *Gautr*, 1–2, *BH*, 1.

GAUTREK, king of West-Gotaland, *Gautr*, 1–2, 5, 8–11, *BH*, 1.

GEIRROD, king of Jotunheim, *Thorst*, 5–11.

GEIRTHJOF, king of the Uplands in Norway, *Gautr*, 3, 5.

GILLING, one of the backwoodsmen, *Gautr*, 1–2.

GLAMMAD, a berserk, *EA*, 10.

GODMUND, king of Glasir Plains, *HB*, 7–8, 10, 12, 14, 16, *Thorst*, 5–12, *HTh*, 1–3.

GORM, earl of Ethiopia, *EA*, 7.

'GRANI HORSE-HAIR', Odin in disguise, *Gautr*, 4, 7.

GRETTIR, one of Vikar's men, *Gautr*, 4.

GUDRUN, daughter of Earl Agdi and wife of Thorstein Mansion-Might, *Thorst*, 11–13.

GUNNOLF BLAZE (G. Blesi), one of Vikar's men, *Gautr*, 4.

GUST, one of Earl Agdi's men, *Thorst*, 6.

HAKON HAMUNDARSON, king of Denmark, *EA*, 18.

HAKON SIGURDARSON, earl of Norway, d. 995, *Thorst*, 1.

HARALD, king of Agder in Norway, *Gautr*, 3–4, 7.

HARALD, king of Wendland, *Gautr*, 8.

HARALD VIKARSSON, ruler of Telemark in Norway, *Gautr*, 5, 9.

HARALD WAR-TOOTH (H. Hilditönn), king of Denmark, *BH*, 1, 9.

HAREK, king of Permia, *BH*, 7–8, 10, 14.

HEIDREK WOLF-SKIN (H. Úlfhéðinn), son of King Godmund, *Thorst*, 12.

HELGA, daughter of King Gautrek and wife of Ref, *Gautr*, 8, 11.

HELGI THORISSON, one of King Olaf Tryggvason's men, *HTh*, 1–3.

HERBRAND, one of Vikar's men, *Gautr*, 4.

HERGRIM, a victim of Starkad, *Gautr*, 7.

HERRAUD, son of King Hring, *BH*, passim.

HERRAUD, son of King Rodian, *EA*, 7, 8, 17.

HERTHJOF, king of Hordaland in Norway, *Gautr*, 3–5.

HERTRYGG, king of Russia, *EA*, 1, 5, 14, 16–18.

HILD, *EA*, 1, 14. See also BEKKHILD and BRYNHILD.

HILDIGRIM, one of Vikar's men, *Gautr*, 4.

HILDIR, uncle of Queen Eagle-Beak, *EA*, 12, 14–16.

HJOTRA, sister and wife of Fjolmond, *Gautr*, 1–2.

HLEID, sister of King Godmund, *BH*, 8, 10, 11, 16.

HOKETIL, a backwoodsman, *BH*, 7, 8, 10.

HOSVIR, one of King Geirrod's men, *Thorst*, 6–7.

HRÆREK, brother of King Rodian, *EA*, 7–8.

HRÆREK, son of King Harek, *BH*, 7, 10–15.

HRING, king of East-Gotaland and father of Herraud, *BH*, 1, 5, 8–11.

HRING, king of the Smalands in Sweden and father of Egil One-Hand, *EA*, 9, 12, 13, 18.

HROLF GAUTREKSSON, the eponymous hero of one of the legendary sagas, *Gautr*, 7.

HROLF KRAKI, the eponymous hero of one of the legendary sagas: *Gautr*, 9–10.
HROSSKEL, one of King Gautrek's men, *Gautr*, 8.
HROTTI, one of Vikar's men, *Gautr*, 4.
HROI, one of Vikar's men, *Gautr*.
HUNTHJOF, king of Hordaland in Norway, *Gautr*, 3.
IMSIGULL, one of the backwoodsmen, *Gautr*, 1–2.
INGIBJORG, mother of Egil One-Hand, *EA*, 9, 12–13, 17.
INGIBJORG, daughter of King Godmund, *HTh*, 1–3.
INGIBJORG THE FAIR, wife of Frithjof the Brave, *Gautr*, 3.
JARNSKEGGI, grandfather of Thorstein Mansion-Might, *Thorst*, 1.
JOKUL, one of Earl Agdi's men, *Thorst*, 6, 9.
JOMALI, pagan deity worshipped in Permia, *BH*, 8–10.
KOLFROSTA, mother of King Harek, *BH*, 8.
KULA, mother of Queen Eagle-Beak, *EA*, 12.
NERI, earl of the Uplands in Norway, *Gautr*, 5, 9–11.
NIGHTFARER (Náttfari), one of King Harald Wartooth's men, *BH*, 1, 9.
ODIN, the god, *Gautr*, 1, 2, 7, *BH*, 1, 12, *EA*, 8, 13, *Thorst*, 3, 9–10.
OLAF THE KEEN-EYED (O. Skyggni), king of Nærike in Sweden, *Gautr*, 5.
OLAF, a warrior king, *Gautr*, 11.
OLAF TRYGGVASON, king of Norway A.D. 995–1000, *Thorst*, 1–2, 4–5, 7–8, 10–12, *HTh*, 1–3.
OSKRUD, father of Queen Eagle-Beak, *EA*, 12, 14.
OTRYGG, a berserk in Sweden, *Gautr*, 7.
OTTAR, earl of Halogaland and father of Asmund Berserks-Killer, *EA*, 6, 18.
OTTAR, earl of Jutland, *EA*, 6.
OTTAR, earl of Novgorod, *Thorst*, 11.
PURSE (Sjóðr), illegitimate son of King Hring, *HB*, 1–4.
RAGNAR HAIRY-BREEKS (R. Loðbrók), the eponymous hero of one of the legendary sagas, *BH*, 9, 16.
REF RENNISON, a farmer's son from Norway, *Gautr*, 6, 9–11.
REF-NOSE (Refnefr), an adviser to King Olaf, *Gautr*, 11.
REGIN, a dwarf, *EA*, 17.
RENNIR, father of Ref, *Gautr*, 6, 9.

RODIAN, king of Tartary, *EA*, 6–7.

ROGNVALD, in charge of King Hertrygg's defences, *EA*, 3, 5.

SEAFARER (Sæfari), earl of the Smalands, *BH*, 1.

SIGGEIR, son of King Harek, *BH*, 7, 10, 11, 13, 14.

SIGGEIR, brother of King Rodian, *EA*, 7, 8.

SIGRID, mother of Asmund Berserks-Killer, *EA*, 6.

SIGURD, a musician at King Godmund's court, *BH*, 11–12.

'SIGURD', Bosi in disguise, *BH*, 12–13.

SIGURD HRING, the eponymous hero of a legendary saga, now lost, *HB*, 9, 16.

SISAR, king of Kiev, *Gautr*, 4.

SKALK, a eunuch, *BH*, 13.

SKIN-BEAK (Skinnefja), daughter of Queen Eagle-Beak, *EA*, 5, 8, 16, 17.

SKINFLINT (Skafnörtungr), one of the backwoodsmen; King Gautrek's grandfather, *Gautr.*, 1–2.

SKJALF, wife of King Agni, *Gautr*, 7.

SKROGG, lawman of the giants, *EA*, 14–16.

SKUMA, one of Vikar's men, *Gautr*, 4.

SMID, brother of Bosi, B.H., 2, 11–14.

SNIDIL, forescastleman on Herraud's ship, *BH*, 14.

SNOTRA (literally 'The Wise One'), mother of Gautrek, *Gautr*, 1–2.

SNOW (Snær), king of the Underworld, *EA*, 13.

SORKVIR, one of Vikar's men, *Gautr*, 4.

STARKAD THE ALA-WARRIOR, grandfather of Starkad the Old, *Gautr*, 3.

STARKAD THE OLD, the tragic hero, *Gautr*, 3–7, *EA*, 18.

STEINTHOR, one of Vikar's men, *Gautr*, 4.

STORVIRK, father of Starkad the Old, *Gautr*, 3, 7.

STUNT-BOSI (Bögu-Bósi), *see* BOSI.

STUNT-BRYNHILD (Brynhildr Baga), *see* BRYNHILD.

STYR, one of Vikar's men, *Gautr*, 4.

SVIDI THE BOLD (S. sókndjarfi), son of Bosi, *BH*, 16.

SYLGJA, mother of Herraud, *BH*, 1.

THOR, the god, *Gautr*, 3, 7, *BH*, 12, *EA*, 12, *Thorst*, 9.

THORA TOWN-HART (þóra borgarhjörtr), wife of Ragnar Hairy-Breeks, *BH*, 16.

THORIR, father of Helgi, *HTh*, 1–3.

THORMOD KARK, Earl Hakon's slave and murderer, *Thorst*, 1.
THORSTEIN MANSION-MIGHT (bæjarmagn) or MANSION-MIDGET (bæjar-
barn), *Thorst*, passim.
THORSTEIN THORISSON, brother of Helgi, *HTh*, 1–2.
THVARI (BRYN-THVARI), father of Bosi, *BH*, 2, 4–6, 11, 14.
TOTRA, wife of Skafnortung, *Gautr*, 1.
ULF, one of Vikar's men, *Gautr*, 4, 5.
ULF, a berserk in Sweden, *Gautr*, 7.
ULFHEDIN TRUSTY, father of King Godmund, *Thorst*, 5.
UNN, mother of Starkad, *Gautr*, 3.
VIKAR, king of Ager in Norway, *Gautr*, 3–7.
VILMUND THE ABSENT-MINDED (V. Viðutan), the eponymous hero of
one of the legendary sagas, *BH*, 16.
VISI, son of Earl Gorm, *EA*, 7, 18.

PLACE NAMES

AGDER, a province in Norway, *Gautr*, 3, 4, 7.
ALFHEIM (in south-east Norway?), *Gautr*, 3.
ALREKSSTEAD, a royal residence in Norway, *HTh*, 2.
ASIA, *BH*, 1.
ASK, a farm on Fenhring Island in Norway, *Gautr*, 4.
BALTIC, *EA*, 10, 18, *Thorst*, 12.
BROW PLAINS (Brávellir), in the south of Sweden, *BH*, 9–10.
DENMARK, *Gautr*, 10, *BH*, 1, *EA*, 6, 18.
DUMB SEA (Dumbshaf), the Arctic regions, *EA*, 15.
EAST GOTALAND, now part of Sweden, *BH*, 1, 8.
ELFAR SKERRIES, off the west coast of Sweden, *BH*, 4.
ENGLAND, *Gautr*, 9.
ETHIOPIA (Blökkumannaland), *EA*, 7.
FAMILY CLIFF (Ætternisstapi), *Gautr*, 1–2.
FINNMARK, in the north of Norway, *HTh*, 1.
FENHRING ISLAND, in Norway, *Gautr*, 4.
GAULARDALE, in Norway, *Thorst*, 1.
GEIRRODSTOWN (Geirröðargarðar), the residence of the mythical King
Geirrod, *Thorst*, 5, 10, 12.

SAXONY, *BH*, 3.
SCANDINAVIA (Norðrlönd), *BH*, 1, 9, *EA*, 18.
SMALANDS, a province in Sweden, *EA*, 9, 12.
STAD, in Norway, *Gautr*, 4.
SVIA SKERRIES (near Stockholm?), *EA*, 10.
SWEDEN, *Gautr*, 1–2, 5, 7.
TARTARY, *EA*, 6, 17–18.
TELEMARK, a province in Norway, *Gautr*, 3, 5, 9.
THRUMA ISLAND, in Norway, *Gautr*, 3, 7.
TRONDHEIM, in Norway, *Thorst*, 12.
UNDERWORLD, a mythical region, *EA*, 12–13, *Thorst*, 2.
UPLANDS, a province in Norway, *Gautr*, 1, 3, 5, 9.
UPPSALA, in Sweden, *Gautr*, 7.
VALHALLA, the home of the heathen gods, *Gautr*, 1–2.
VÆNER, a lake in Sweden, *Gautr*, 4.
VIKARS ISLAND, in Norway, *Gautr*, 7.
VIMUND, a headland in Norway, *HTh*, 1.
VINA FOREST, in Permia, *BH*, 7, 10.
WENDLAND, *Gautr*, 8.
WEST GOTALAND, now part of Sweden, *Gautr*, 1.
YRJAR, a district in Norway, *Thorst*, 1.